SANCTUS FUMIGACI

Collected Works Volume 2:
Short Plays

by Todd Bash

© 2006 Todd Bash *First Edition*
© 2021 Todd Bash *Second Edition*
All Rights Reserved

No part of this publication may be reproduced, stored in a retrieval system or transmitted in any form or by any means, electronic, mechanical, photocopying, recording or otherwise.

The plays contained in this volume are fully protected by copyright and may not be performed or read for an audience without prior permission from the author in writing.

Inquires concerning possible amateur or professional productions should be made to the author in care of *Nachthunde Publishing*, or to the author's representative at the following email address: bashkiewicz@aol.com

ISBN: 978-1-7376525-0-2

Publications by Todd Bash

Collected Works Vol. 1: Early Plays
(*The Winning Number, Concrete and Blackouts*)

Sanctus Fumigaci
Collected Works Vol. 2: Short Plays
(*Das Nachtgespenst, Goldring – The First Generation, Nachthunde, Mondvögel, The Final Thoughts of Stanislaw Bashkiewicz, The Last of the Living Surrealists, The Hobo Screenplay, and Seehunde*)

Final Thoughts
Published by Broken Boulder Press, 2001
(including *The Final Thoughts of Tatala Bashkiewicz, The Final Dream of Tatala Bashkiewicz, The Second to Last Dream of Tatala Bashkiewicz, The Final Thoughts of Todd Bash* and *Epitaph*.)

Neotrope #1
Published by Broken Boulder Press, 2000
(Collection of experimental writing including *Das Nachtgespenst*)

Forthcoming from Nachthunde Publishing

The Final Thoughts of Tatala Bashkiewicz
Plays, Poetry and Prose

The Last of the Living Surrealists & Other Blasphemous Works
A collaboration by Todd Bash & Gustavo Octavio

Contents

Das Nachtgespenst | 1

Goldring – The First Generation | 45

Nachthunde | 93

Mondvögel | 117

The Final Thoughts of Stanislaw Bashkiewicz | 125

APPENDIX: COLLABORATIONS | 137

The Last of the Living Surrealists | 139

The Hobo Screenplay | 153

Seehunde | 167

Das Nachtgespenst

A Love Story
(1991)

Characters

Michael
Gustavo
Andrea
Carl
Charles
Dean
François
Fat John

Special Appearances by...

Kurt Gerron
Luis Buñuel
Anna Bronski
Paul Eluard
Oliver Reed
Bertolt Brecht

As well as additional minor characters.

Notes:

In an early production, the main character's name, for unexplained reasons, was changed to Joey. For the second edition, it has now been restored to its original name, Michael.

The songs *Das Nachtgespenst* and *Verborgenheit* have been translated from the original German.

Verborgenheit translation by Gustavo Jimenez.

1

The jazz of Mister John Coltrane, June 28, 1965. The place stinks of urine, feels of heat and looks of red.

Enter MICHAEL.

Pause.

He remembers ANDREA for one minute, then notices a lump in his carpeting.

Pause.

He slowly lifts the corner of the carpet, revealing a soft, naked corpse. She's decomposing.

2

The radio dial changes to *News* 98. Charles Bartly reports:

...And the rash of suicides continues to plague the Southland as forty more deaths were reported through the night. The toll now is more than eight hundred, the majority caused by self-inflicted gun shot wounds to the head. With us now is biologist Henri Laborit, a leading analyst of human behavior. Tell us doctor, what is your opinion as to why this bizarre tragedy is happening?...

3

MICHAEL: **BOO HOO HOO HOO! BOO HOO HOO HOO! BOO HOO HOO HOO! BOO HOO HOO HOO!**

CHARLES: What's the matter with him?

MICHAEL: **BOO HOO HOO HOO!**

DEAN: He's got a rock on his head.

CHARLES: A what?

DEAN: A rock on his head.

(MICHAEL removes a baseball cap, displaying a piece of granite growing from his skull.)

CHARLES: That's no problem. I've cured those millions of times. It's easy.

MICHAEL: You have?

CHARLES: Certainly. Right, Dean? (He gives an obvious wink and hand gesture to DEAN.) First, I need a poker. (He grabs a thin, steel rod.) This will do. Now, some heat. (He removes the shade from a lamp and proceeds to hold the end of the poker against the hot light bulb.)

Silence.

(A fireplace is rolled into the room.)

CHARLES: Ah, perfect. (He sets the poker in the fireplace and grabs a handful of ashes. He sprinkles the ashes in Joey's hair, then massages firmly. Dust and powder clouds the air as MICHAEL lets out a cough. Charles returns to his poker, carefully holding it to the heat.)

Silence.

CHARLES: Here. I'm not sure it's ready yet. Test 'er out.

Pause.

(MICHAEL moves slowly toward CHARLES.)

Pause.

(CHARLES lifts the poker and presses the end of it against Michael's cheek. A loud sizzling sound is heard.)

Pause.

CHARLES: How's she feel?

MICHAEL: I'm not sure.

CHARLES: Does it hurt?

MICHAEL: Sort of.

(*Silence*, as CHARLES continues to hold the poker against Michael's cheek.)

CHARLES: Okay. Let's operate. (He removes the poker, now placing it on Michael's head, firmly pressing against the granite. Again, a loud sizzling sound is heard.)

Silence.

(Enter GUSTAVO. He carries a small plastic bag containing ash, liquid and pieces of dead cockroach.)

GUSTAVO: I've done a liquid test on the ash. It's clear to see what's causing your problem.

CHARLES: Of course. Just as I suspected.

DEAN: Don't fret, Mike. It happens to billions everyday. Common medicine.

CHARLES: Right. (*Pause.*) You're not frightened, are you? (*Pause.*) Relax.

Silence.

MICHAEL: Oh. Oh. ***OHHHHHHHHHHHHHHHH!!!!!!!***

(The granite burns from Michael's head. It falls to the floor, followed by many roaches pouring from his brain.)

BLACKOUT.

The curtain lowers.

4

KURT GERRON sings "Das Nachtgespenst" or "The Night Ghost", March 18, 1929. A showgirl points out the English translation opposite stage.

THE NIGHT GHOST

When the housewife closes the door
I'm standing silently in the hallway.
With my file, without shame
I break it away, it falls in the filth.
And when the daughter undresses for bed
I'm sorry to say, I enter her room.

I am the night ghost
Your sweet little night ghost
I wake you up from your night prayer
So often that I'll call you sweetheart.

Don't be frightened or worried
I'm only uncovering your bed sheets
And once I've removed all of your sheets
I'll cover you up once more.

When I climb in through the window
It's not jewels that provoke me
No – It's only your ivory skin!
As a night ghost I don't take
Anything that sparkles.
The only thing I really need
Is my return fare.

In the press they say I cause agony,
A scandal and that I'm not normal.
I am so overcome with sadness
That I go home and cry.
In the day time I am a government worker,
And only at night do I get into mischief.

I am the night ghost
Your sweet little night ghost
I wake you up from your night prayer
So often that I'll call you sweetheart.
Etc...

Applause.

BLACKOUT.

5

(MICHAEL appears on a stool. He speaks directly to the audience about Andrea.)

MICHAEL: I first met Andrea in a poetry course at the university. From across the room she seemed remarkably sexy. Her body created an energy, a sense of aggressiveness, which I found exciting. She was clearly older and more experienced than I was. The first time I saw her up close I was rather surprised. Her face was simple. She wore no make-up. Her eyes were gentle, and her nose had tiny freckles on its sides. The contrast between her soft innocence and her aggressive sensuality was striking. I remember attempting to spark up a conversation with her. She began telling me...

During the previous sentence, Michael's monologue and image begin to fade into the background. His words become slightly more than mumbles; his appearance becomes dimly lit. Instead, the focus is now on FRANÇOIS, opposite stage. François' upcoming monologue and the remainder of Michael's monologue are performed simultaneously, but, again, the focus is clearly on FRANÇOIS. The effect should be the equivalent of a dream or memory entering one's consciousness, while exterior reality fades into a barely audible background. Since the remainder of Michael's monologue is barely heard, the actor is hereby given freedom to improvise dialogue. Michael's story, however, should at least partially parallel the following outline:

1. While Michael finds himself attracted to Andrea, he also fears she may be somewhat "normal" for him. In turn, Andrea does not display any signs of physical attraction toward Michael.

2. During the following months, Michael periodically fantasizes

about fucking Andrea. He does not act on his desire, and the two remain classmates, nothing more.

3. After their poetry class has ended, Michael does not see Andrea for more than a year. The two ultimately bump into one another at a Dalí exhibit at the museum. Andrea reveals to Michael how his discussions in class inspired her to explore the Surrealists in 1920's Paris. She has since exposed herself to the artistic works of Buñuel, Dalí, Magritte, and Lorca, among others. She shares some of her poetry with Michael. The two proceed in developing a close friendship.

4. On the dawn of becoming lovers, Andrea's former boyfriend, Carl, reenters her life. He proposes, and the two become engaged. Michael continues playing the role of friend, though he secretly awaits another chance to become Andrea's lover.

5. Andrea and Carl end their relationship. Michael and Andrea become lovers.

6. Once again, Carl enters Andrea's life. Ultimately, Andrea ends her relationship with Michael and returns to Carl. She claims she deeply cares for Michael, but can never stop loving Carl, no matter how screwed-up he is. Michael is shattered.

Opposite stage, FRANÇOIS performs his monologue. The monologue is spoken in French. An interpreter translates for the audience.

FRANÇOIS: I could see her standing in the hallway, naked and unbathed. Neither of us had bathed in more than a month. The stench from our bodies seemed unsettling at first, but in time, we simply didn't smell it.

Her hair was oily. She had small flakes on the tips of her eyelids. I found her a complete image of beauty.

Her breasts were soft and sweet. Her eyes brown and melancholy. I felt complete love inside me. The air was flooded by love.

Together, we had become uninhibited. I felt at ease, open, uncensored, as if I were alone, by myself.

Both of us could do anything in front of the other. There were no fears, no embarrassment.

Crap, fart, masturbate, urinate, burp, itch, snort, smell, moan, giggle, cry...it didn't matter. We were completely comfortable in each other's presence.

She entered my room. Her softness. I gently brushed my fingers against her face. She smiled, then joined me under the covers. We firmly grasped one another. I pressed my flesh inside her, but didn't fuck. I remained still, resting, the two of us as one, completely overwhelmed by our passion.

I remained inside of her for much of the evening. I slept, but didn't dream. My mind and body were transformed into a statue of absolute pleasure and tranquility.

In the morning, I was awakened by an odd, grinding sound. I discovered my loved one had left my arms. I opened the blind, noticing a giant cow in my yard, munching on a tree.

(A cowbell is heard. It continues throughout the remainder of the monologue.)

I searched the room for my loved one. I called for her by name.
JEANNE! JEANNE!
I searched the yard.
She was nowhere to be found.

During the following months, I filed a missing persons report. I waited by the phone. I never saw my Jeanne again.

(The cowbell continues for several seconds.)

BLACKOUT.

6

The Prelude from Wagner's *Tristan und Isolde* is heard. Enter ANDREA, who elegantly dances. Her body movement is soft and innocent, yet somehow sensual and passionate. After a moment, the Prelude nears its conclusion. Lights fade on ANDREA. Simultaneously, lights up on MICHAEL, who remains alone.

Silence.

BLACKOUT.

7

The sounds of a train raging underground are heard. MICHAEL and GUSTAVO ride public transportation.

GUSTAVO: I had a dream last night. I dreamed the Nazis conquered Manhattan. I was on 14th Street. The sky was almost entirely gray, but had glimpses of color. The buildings were completely brown. In fact, everything was brown: clothes, cars. It was almost like black and white, but not really. I was standing in a long line of people outside my building. I felt frightened. I was sweating. I asked someone what was happening. A large man struck me. He told me to shut up. I noticed giant red flags flying atop the city.

(ANDREA enters slowly. After a pause-)

MICHAEL: I dreamed of her today. I dreamed the streets were completely flooded. Like shallow lakes. I was swimming. I heard a plane flying low overhead. It began dropping bombs…

(In addition to subway sounds, a World War II fighter plane is now heard. One by one, the plane drops three bombs, which explode in water. The combination of subway sounds and plane sounds completely drowns out anything spoken by MICHAEL. Once the plane sounds have ended, MICHAEL and GUSTAVO become silent. The train continues raging underground. It enters a tunnel, as green lights quickly flash through the windows.)

BLACKOUT.

8

The sounds of horses sneezing are vaguely heard. MICHAEL and GUSTAVO wander the city. A collection of faces appears.

Silence.

MICHAEL: Look at these people. They're dead. They're completely emotionless. (*Pause.*) Don't they have any conscience?

FACE #1 (begins laughing): Ho ho ho. He he he. Ho ho ho. He he he.

GUSTAVO: What the hell is he laughing about? There's nothing funny here.

FACE #2: OH HO HO HO! OH HO HO HO! OH HO HO HO!

MICHAEL: Shut up! There's nothing to laugh about!

FACE #3: AH HA HA HA! AH HA HA HA! AH HA HA HA!

(The faces continue laughing. A fourth face presents a silent laugh: His head bobs backward and forward - mouth open, eyes shut - as if laughing, but no sound is actually heard.)

MICHAEL: I said shut up! Stop laughing! STOP LAUGHING!

(After a moment, the faces slightly fade into the background. Like in Scene Five, the aim is to create the effect of a passing dream or memory entering one's consciousness, while a previous thought fades out of focus. In this case, a memory is performed opposite stage. MICHAEL and GUSTAVO observe as three young boys, one of whom is MICHAEL as a ten year old, pass the hours on a lazy afternoon.)

FIRST BOY: Check these out, man. (He removes two rifles from under his bed.)

SECOND BOY: Woe! Those're bad!

FIRST BOY: You wanna shoot people?

SECOND BOY: Yeah!!

LITTLE MICHAEL: Um...guys...I don't...

(Enter FAT JOHN. He wobbles as if his inner thighs are desperately chafed. His flesh is pale, with spots of red.)

FIRST BOY: *HEY! IT'S FAT JOHN! LET'S GET 'IM!*

SECOND BOY: *COOL!*

(The FIRST BOY and the SECOND BOY kneel before a window, quietly pointing their rifles in the direction of FAT JOHN.)

LITTLE MICHAEL (frightened): Guys...I don't think...I mean that's cold. Don't do it. Come on, man. Knock it off. That's *cold.* Don't...

(The boys shoot FAT JOHN.)

FAT JOHN: Ow!

(He quickly grabs his arm. Then, suddenly, a painful squeal erupts-) *WAAAAAAAAAAAAAAAAAAAAAAAAAAAAAA AAAAAAAAAAAAAAA!!!!!!!!!!!!!!!!!!!!!!!!!!!!!!!!!!!*

(The three boys burst with laughter. They rock cartoonishly, forward and backward, firmly holding their aching tummies.)

BOYS: *AH HA HA HA! AH HA HA HA! AH HA HA HA!*

FAT JOHN (crying): Quit throwin' rocks!

(The faces return to the foreground. The space is now overwhelmed by laughter.)

AH HA HA HA! AH HA HA HA!
HO HO HO! HE HE HE! AH HA HA HA!

MICHAEL: It's not funny. They just shot him! Why am I laughing! Stop it! STOP LAUGHING! *STOP LAUGHING!!*

AH HA HA HA! AH HA HA HA!
HO HO HO! HE HE HE! AH HA HA HA!

(Enter a STRANGER.)

STRANGER: Pst. Pst. Hey you. Over here.

MICHAEL: Me?

STRANGER: Yeah you. You want some BBs? Come on. You remember. They bounce off your flesh. Sting like a son of a bitch. Don't do no serious damage, though.

MICHAEL: Hm.

STRANGER: You take these babies, go on the roof 'cross the street from 'er place. Pump pump. Don't really hurt 'er, see, just sting the shit out of 'er arms.

MICHAEL (interested): Yeah.

STRANGER: Just poke 'er like a needle or somethin'. She'll figure a bee's out ta get 'er ev'ry time she goes for the car.

MICHAEL (excited): *Yeah!*

STRANGER: You hear what I'm sayin'?

MICHAEL: I do.

STRANGER: I'll arrange it you can get on my friend's roof 'cross the street.

(The STRANGER hands the BBs to MICHAEL who, after a moment's contemplation, lets out a fiendish smile. The laughing continues.)

AH HA HA HA! AH HA HA HA!
HO HO HO! HE HE HE! AH HA HA HA!

BLACKOUT.

9

Lights slowly rise on MICHAEL and ANDREA.

Silence.

MICHAEL: I don't want you to go back to him. (*Pause.*) I want to love you.

Silence.

10

Soft piano is heard. After a moment, enter GUSTAVO, who sings *Verborgenheit,* a piece of German lieder music by Hugo Wolf.

VERBORGENHEIT

Leave me alone O World, Oh let me be
Do not tempt me with the gifts of love.
Let this heart alone feel its bliss, its pain.
What I grieve, I'm not sure
It's unknown misery.
Always through these tears do I see the sun's dear light.
Often I am hardy conscious
And the bright joy quivers through the heaviness
Until, with deep pressure, my breast feels the supreme delight.
Leave me alone O World, Oh let me be
Do not tempt me with the gifts of love.
Let this heart alone feel its bliss, its pain.

11

After a pause, CHARLES appears on a stool. He speaks directly to the audience.

CHARLES: Michael told Andrea he wouldn't call her for two weeks. Andrea had claimed she needed time to sort things out by herself. They both knew she was simply postponing the inevitable. On Thursday, Michael fled the city for a mountain in Mexico. The guerrilla soldiers drew near as the revolution reached its height in bloodshed. The screams of anarchy sliced into the cemetery...

12

A cemetery, July 29, 1993. An explosion is heard, followed by the sounds of distant gunfire. LUIS BUÑUEL appears, emerging from a coffin. He stretches gloriously after a decade-long nap.

Enter MICHAEL.

BUÑUEL: Hola.

MICHAEL: Hello.

BUÑUEL: I see you've brought the items I requested. Gracias. (MICHAEL hands BUÑUEL a bottle of red wine and a glass. BUÑUEL pours, then drinks.) Ah! That feels good!

(BUÑUEL sets the alcohol aside. MICHAEL then hands him a large collection of newspapers, magazines and journals.)

BUÑUEL: Let me see now...(He begins browsing through a newspaper.) War...oppression...hypocrisy...murder... disease... famine...revolution. It seems the more things change the more they stay the same. (He tosses the newspaper aside, then begins reading a journal.) Hm. Is it really true my films are readily available on video throughout most of the world?

MICHAEL: Absolutely.

BUÑUEL: Even *Las Hurdes*?

MICHAEL: Yes.

BUÑUEL: Incredible. (He continues reading.) Well...I've seen enough. I guess I'll be getting back now.

MICHAEL: So soon?

BUÑUEL: I'm not as strong as I used to be. I want you to know, though, I consider you a remarkably lucky person.

MICHAEL: Really?

BUÑUEL: Of course. *You're here!* There is more going on in the world today than ever before. Technological change is occurring every *instant!* You see, I had to leave in the middle. I'm missing the most exciting part. But you...You should be grateful for the opportunities you're given.

(Once again, an explosion is heard. The fighting draws nearer as the cries of "CUIDADO CON LA CARTERA!" echo the space.)

BUÑUEL: So long, my atheist friend. I'll see you in another ten years.

(BUÑUEL returns to his coffin. He begins fluffing a pillow, preparing for his long rest. Meanwhile, a PEASANT appears, frantically fleeing a gang of bandits. Suddenly, a blast is heard. The PEASANT falls to the ground. The bandits enter and swipe the peasant's wallet and shoes. After a pause-)

BUÑUEL (smiles): I envy you.

(BUÑUEL retires peacefully. His face displays an expression of contentment, a sense of safeness and security as he naps inside his tomb. The space by this time has begun erupting into an anarchistic frenzy. In addition to explosions and gunfire, an OLD WOMAN is seen praying to Jesus while a group of thugs brutally stone her.)

OLD WOMAN: *JESUS CRISTO SALVA ME!*

(The sounds of a helicopter are now heard. Its searchlight scans the space, finally focusing on a spot center stage. The following command is heard through a bullhorn from the helicopter: *"SACA LAS MANOS DE TUS PANTALONES! DE NUEVO: SACA LAS MANOS DE TUS PANTALONES!"* After a moment, the helicopter sounds fade, though the searchlight center stage remains. An air raid siren begins. It continues for several seconds before fading. Ultimately, the space becomes completely silent. Only the searchlight is seen...

13

MICHAEL and ANDREA are heard.

MICHAEL: Mmm. I love your breasts. I love everything about you. (*Pause*.) Your legs are so beautiful. Your ass is the most magnificent creation on the face of the earth. There isn't another woman whose ass compares with yours. And I'd say this even if I had complete emotional detachment and didn't love you. There's simply no question. (*Pause*.) Mmmmmmmmmmm. Your pussy is stupendous. It's pure perfection.
(*Pause*.)
I like to stick my tongue inside your bellybutton and taste you. You're so sweet and gentle.
(*Pause*.)
I love making love to you.

(Enter ANNA BRONSKI, grandmother of Oskar Matzerath from the Gunter Grass novel *The Tin Drum*. This is the woman who, at the turn of the century, while in a potato field, harbored a fugitive under her skirt. She grabs ANDREA by the hair and drags her on stage.)

ANNA: Bitch! Whore! You don't deserve to be part of his life! (Dragging ANDREA by the hair in one hand, ANNA exits, then returns, pushing a barrel of water.) You don't care about him. His affection toward you is unreturned. (She exits, then returns, this time pulling MICHAEL by his ear. She places MICHAEL'S hands around Andrea's neck, then pushes Andrea's head into the barrel of water.) Go ahead. Drown her. Destroy her thoughts once and for all.

MICHAEL: No.

ANNA: She doesn't care about you. She pushed you into the water when you needed shelter from those lunatics. **She fucks other toads!**

MICHAEL: No.

ANNA: **She eats other meat!** Now kill her and end it.

MICHAEL: No!

ANNA: I said *drown her!* **DROWN HER! DROWN HER!** (She pushes Andrea's head under the water.) **DROWN HER! DROWN HER!**

MICHAEL: *No!* **NO!**
    (*Silence.*)
    (to Andrea): I love you.
    (*Brief pause.*)
    Tell me you love me.

ANDREA: I love you, Michael. I want us to spend the rest of our lives together. I want you to make love to me every night. I adore you.

(Enter GUSTAVO. His ass has grown to more than five feet long and drags across the stage floor. With a hammer, GUSTAVO pounds a wooden crutch into the floor. He flips his ass atop the crutch, gaining support, then kneels, placing his chin on his fist in a thinking position. After a pause-)

MICHAEL: I'm an idiot. It was all in my mind, wasn't it? She doesn't care about me. She never did.
(to ANDREA): I hate you. I'm coughing blood and you're not here. You betrayed me. I hope you get AIDS and suffer the way I am.
Bitch! (He dunks Andrea's head under the water, then lets go.) I can't do it. I'm a pussy.
(to GUSTAVO): You're laughing at me, aren't you? I've become the equivalent of a born again Christian.
I'm all heart and no logic.
I disgust myself.
(*Silence.*)
(to ANDREA): I still want you. Tell me how I can get you to love me.
I love you, Andrea.

Silence.

DONG! DONG! DONG!

14

A synagogue. The sound of a grandfather clock "donging" is heard. In addition, the clock's "tick tock" cuts into a silence that envelops the space. MICHAEL stands alone.

Enter ANDREA. She moves the hands on the grandfather clock up one hour. The time now reads *three o'clock*.

DONG! DONG! DONG!

Again, ANDREA moves the hands on the clock, this time up two hours. The time reads *five o'clock*.

DONG! DONG! DONG!

Silence.

MICHAEL leaves the synagogue. A slight change in lighting suggests he has made his way outdoors. The "tick tock" fades, as the sounds of children playing are now heard.

Enter a young couple who begin setting up a table and chairs. They are preparing for a bagel and donut sale. MICHAEL observes quietly.

After a moment, MICHAEL notices an unfolded, portable table, which is unattended. He begins to drag it slowly across the space.

Enter a WOMAN in her late sixties. She follows MICHAEL, giving him disconcerting glances.

WOMAN (mumbling): What disrespect!

Silence.

The sounds of children playing begin to fade. MICHAEL is now in a deserted school yard.

Silence.

MICHAEL eyes the area cluelessly. He lifts his hand slowly and hypnotically stares into it. Green blood begins oozing from the center of Michael's palm. After a pause -

MICHAEL: Holy shit. I've got gangrene.

BLACKOUT.

15

A brief montage of thoughts is presented, beginning with a slight exchange between ELIZABETH and TOM.

ELIZABETH: Whata ya think I am? A fucking whore?!

TOM: I put my *life* into this relationship. How can you do this to me?!

(The focus now shifts to ANDREA, who is opposite stage.)

ANDREA: I'm dreaming. Small brown leaves gently blow across my bed. I can feel them brushing against my skin. I suddenly realize my breasts have grown...large, beautiful and firm.

(Enter the poet PAUL ELUARD.)

ELUARD: Don't torture me. How can I live another minute knowing I'll never again touch your skin? I beg you. My beautiful angel, my magnificent treasure of flesh and spirit. My only pleasure these days is staring at your naked photos, where your breasts are moist enough to drink, where your stomach breathes in and out and I taste it with my tongue, before swallowing it whole. Your legs are spread wide open over my longing face, then my prick plunges deep inside, as I caress your beautiful ass, which moves marvelously, like the earth itself. You have the most stunning brown eyes I have ever seen. I am so in love with you. You clutch my prick in your hand, your body quivering, you jerk me off furiously, I dig into your breasts, your hair, and suddenly your whole arm is covered in my fluids and you're sure of the spell I've cast over you, of the spell you've cast over me, of *everything!* Ohhhhhhhhhh. My magnificent flower. Don't leave me behind...

(Enter MICHAEL.)

MICHAEL: Get over her, man. I mean she doesn't love you anymore. She loves *him.* (He slaps ELUARD across his face.) Stop acting like such a pathetic weakling!

(GUSTAVO enters, running across the stage, his ass still dragging against the floor.)

GUSTAVO: *SUSAN! SUSAN!* (He stops, lifting his excess rear blubber in his arms, then continues running.) **SUSAN! I LOVE YOU!**

(MICHAEL and ELUARD, puzzled, glance at one another.)

BLACKOUT.

16

DONG! DONG! DONG! DONG!

The "donging" continues throughout the following monologue. FRANÇOIS appears. As in *Scene Five,* he speaks in French. An interpreter translates for the audience.

FRANÇOIS: In my mind I remember everything. I remember the moments I could have acted, but didn't. And how my life may have been different if I had. I remember my shame, my embarrassment, as I disgracefully tried anything to recapture love. Even praying to God. I remember brief spaces in time, instants, when I actually thought my hope was becoming real. For only a breath, I believed in us. Something I still haven't been able to forget.

DONG! DONG! DONG! DONG!

(In addition to "donging," a telephone is heard ringing. It sounds three times before someone answers.)

17

A telephone conversation between MICHAEL and ANDREA is heard.

MICHAEL: Hello?...Hello?

Pause.

ANDREA: It's me. (*Silence.*)

I just wanted to talk with you.
I don't know...
I wanted to apologize for standing you up when...
you know...

Silence.

MICHAEL: Are you okay?

ANDREA: Yeah. (She begins crying.) Carl and I broke up. It's over between us.

Silence.

MICHAEL: I don't know what to say.

ANDREA: He hurt me really bad, Michael. I'd like to hurt him right now. (*Pause.*)
I guess it's been coming for months.
I just want to forget about him.
(*Pause.*) Could you come over?

Silence.

MICHAEL: I don't know if that's a good idea.

ANDREA: Please. I feel so much better when you're here. (*Pause.*) I'm sorry for the way I treated you. I realize now how much I care for you. You were the one who was always there for me. I'd really like to be with you tonight. Please.

Silence.

MICHAEL: I guess I could come over. I'm sort of in the middle of something right now. How about in an hour?

ANDREA: Can you make it sooner? I'd really like to see you.

Pause.

MICHAEL: How about in fifteen minutes?

ANDREA: Good.

MICHAEL: Okay...I'll see you in fifteen minutes then.

ANDREA: I'll be waiting. Hurry. (She kisses the phone.)

MICHAEL: Bye.

(MICHAEL hangs up. A dial tone is heard. It continues for several seconds before slowly fading.)

18

Once again, FRANÇOIS speaks to the audience.

FRANÇOIS: When I sleep, she appears in my dreams. She appears in my bed every night. I can feel her breath against my chest. When I rest in the school yard, she appears on the swings. She appears in stores. In buildings. On the freeway, her face reflects in every side view mirror in traffic. I realize she is no longer a person. She is purely a ghost that has taken up residence inside of me. My guts and brain are completely dominated by her image.

19

MICHAEL and ANDREA say good-bye.

ANDREA: I want to be friends. I don't want...I want us to be the way we were before. Do you understand?

Pause.

MICHAEL: I can't just erase these feelings inside of me. I mean...

ANDREA: Well...

MICHAEL: I mean I care for you.

ANDREA: Forget it. Just forget it then. I think it's better if we no longer see each other for awhile. (*Pause.*) Don't call me anymore.

MICHAEL: Not at all? (*Pause.*) Can I at least call to see if you're okay now and then?

ANDREA: No. No. Under no circumstances...*Do not call me*...I think its better this way.

Silence.

MICHAEL: So...Are you saying you don't love me? You never will?
(*Silence.*)
Go ahead.
Tell me.

Silence.

ANDREA: I can't answer that question.

(Enter the actor OLIVER REED. He pauses, then passionately, yet precisely, recites a line from the D.H. Lawrence novel *Women in Love-)*

OLIVER REED: Why do you torture me?

(*Pause*, then Mister Reed turns, bends, and lets out a monstrous fart!)

MUSIC!

20

Enter MICHAEL in a clown suit. He masterfully performs an excerpt from Leoncavallo's opera *Pagliacci,* only he substitutes for the actual libretto the words, "Poochie Puppy, Kitty Wittie, Holyshitarolly."

GUSTAVO: Good. Good. You'll do fine. Don't stress it.

MICHAEL: But I don't even know what opera we're performing. How will I know what to sing?

GUSTAVO: Look. I set up a prompter offstage right. Just read the libretto and improv.

MICHAEL: But I'll look silly always staring offstage right.
(GUSTAVO exits.)
How about...What if we move the moon stage right? That way the audience will think I'm staring into the moonlight.
(He notices GUSTAVO has left.)

Gustavo? Gustavo?
(Enter a young woman.)
Have you seen Gustavo?
I need the moon moved stage right.
(The young woman completely ignores MICHAEL.)
Gustavo? *Gustavo?!*

(GUSTAVO reenters, eating from a plate of Spaghetti Os.)

GUSTAVO (his mouth is full): *What?!*

MICHAEL: I want the moon moved stage right!

GUSTAVO: Would ya stop stressin'. Ev'rything's gonna be fine.

MICHAEL: I don't even know my character's name yet! **I'M NOT SURE WHO I'LL BE PERFORMING WITH!**

GUSTAVO: Relax. You'll meet her in a minute. Listen. She's ready to begin rehearsing.

(The sounds of the great Birgit Nilsson performing the Liebestod from Wagner's *Tristan und Isolde* are heard. MICHAEL and GUSTAVO listen in awe.)

MICHAEL: Is that her?

(GUSTAVO smiles tenderly and nods his head up and down. The two continue listening. As the music reaches its height-)

MICHAEL: My god. She's not human.

(Others join onstage. Everyone is deeply moved by the heavenly voice. The composition peacefully reaches its conclusion.)

LIGHTS SLOWLY FADE TO DARKNESS.

Silence.

21

King Crimson's *Larks' Tongues in Aspic, part two* (recorded live) is heard. It continues throughout the following scene. MICHAEL appears on a roof top, carefully plotting an assault. He removes a rifle, then begins loading. Enter ANDREA and CARL. MICHAEL aims the rifle. *Pause.* He fires.

ANDREA: Ow! (She grabs her arm.)

CARL: What happened?

ANDREA: Something stung me. I'm in terrible pain.

(Again, MICHAEL fires.)

ANDREA: OW!

CARL: What?

ANDREA: It got me again. A bee or something. It hurts so bad.

CARL: Let me see. (He examines Andrea's arm.) It's red alright. I didn't see anything flying, though.

(MICHAEL reloads, once again takes aim, then fires.)

CARL: *OHHHHHHHHHHHHHHHHHHHHHHHHH!!!!!!!!!!!*

(CARL is shot in the face. Blood pours from his eye.)

CARL: MY EYE!

ANDREA: Oh my god!

(CARL falls to the ground.)

CARL: Shit! SHIT! *OHHHHHHHHHHHHHH!!!!!!!!!!!!!!!*

(MICHAEL, absolutely shocked, hurriedly gathers his arsenal. Enter a beautiful young woman to the roof top.)

WOMAN: What happened?

MICHAEL: I shot him in the eye. It was an accident, though. It was supposed to just bounce off his arm. Oh fuck.

WOMAN: Don't worry. He deserved it. He's a punk. There has to be some justice now and then. We certainly can't rely on god. Here. (She takes MICHAEL by his hand.) Come and make love to me.

MICHAEL: You're beautiful. (*Pause.*)
It's useless, though. I can't even fantasize about other women. The moment we begin to screw you'll just turn into her.

CARL: *OHHHHHHHHHHHHHHHHHHHHHHHHH!!!!!!!!!*

WOMAN: Maybe you should at least try.

Pause.

BLACKOUT.

22

The radio dial changes to a far off channel.
Nuremberg, 1923. Julius Streicher passionately gives a speech.
Enter KURT GERRON.

GERRON: I performed alongside Emil Jannings once. They said the two of us were terrific together. He later called me subhuman and supported those who were responsible for murdering me.

(Enter the playwright BERTOLT BRECHT who, in German, recites the following-)

BRECHT: The modern theater mustn't be judged by its success in satisfying the audience's habits, but by its success in transforming them. It needs to be questioned not about its degree of conformity with the eternal laws of the theater, but about its ability to master the rules governing the great social processes of our age; not about whether it manages to interest the spectator in buying a ticket - i.e. in the theater itself - but about whether it manages to interest him in the world.

(During Brecht's statement, the following conversation occurs between KURT GERRON and MICHAEL.)

GERRON: Brecht. Son of a bitch. He'd screw his own mother.

MICHAEL: He's the greatest playwright in the history of theater. He's a genius.

GERRON: He constantly poked fun at me. "Without your fat belly you couldn't make a living," he said. Bastard. Yet he survived. I was murdered by those filthy cocksuckers. You can't trust anyone.

(The sounds of Julius Streicher continue.)

BLACKOUT.

23

CHARLES speaks directly to the audience.

CHARLES: And so Michael made his way through the icyed acorns toward Andrea, who was lying flat on a stone, her legs spread wide open as her fingers tickled the lips of her mighty friend.
(MICHAEL'S voice): "I see you," whispered Michael. His arms desperately reached toward Andrea's milk. His fingers, as if they had a mind of their own, wiggled toward her lips. But just before Michael could feel...(The sounds of a storm are heard.)...a storm flooded the forest, drowning his image in an ocean of sores. Underwater, Michael slowly moved among the scavengers of the sea, most of whom were hard-shelled creatures who lived on the shit from others. (*Brief pause.*) After a moment of shame, Michael swam to the surface, where he coughed on the air, before spiraling into another dream...

(Enter MICHAEL.)

MICHAEL: I dreamed my life had ended. Like Trotsky, who got an ax in his skull, and Lorca, who got two bullets in his ass for being queer, my thoughts were murdered by the terrorists of logic. They shot my tires, causing me to crash. (The sounds of a car crashing are heard. A loud explosion follows, as well as the crackling of fire, which continues throughout the remainder of the scene.) The moon began bleeding. The clouds smelled of urine. I could feel the unraveling of my skin as it anxiously crawled from my torso. My brain then became empty. I no longer had thoughts. I was suddenly a hollow, cold creature, free, changing into nothing. I simply burned. Sizzling and curling...like a piece of paper.

(MICHAEL removes a piece of paper and lights it on fire. He watches, as the paper curls and burns. After a moment, he drops it in a tin container on the floor. The paper continues burning. MICHAEL exits.)

LIGHTS SLOWLY FADE.

(The glow from the fire is seen for several seconds.)

24

The jazz of Mister John Coltrane, June 28, 1965. MICHAEL is found deep in thought. He then discovers a lump in his carpeting.

Pause.

He slowly lifts the corner of the carpet, revealing a soft, naked corpse.

Pause.

MICHAEL kneels. He gently strokes the corpse's hair. He then kisses her mouth, followed by her breasts.

Silence.

MICHAEL begins making love to the corpse. He pulls the carpeting over himself and his lover.

LIGHTS SLOWLY FADE TO BLACK.

The music of John Coltrane continues...

DAS NACHTGESPENST   39

Biographical notes on historical and artistic figures who appear, or are referred to, in the play.

BERTOLT BRECHT.
Born 1898 in Augsburg, Germany. Died 1956.
A revolutionary poet and playwright, Brecht established many of the theories and conventions associated with *epic theater*. Among his finest plays are A Man's A Man, Galileo, and Mother Courage and Her Children. Brecht fled Germany in 1933 after Hitler's rise to power. He lived in California during the 1940's, but returned to Europe in 1947 following his appearance before the House Committee on Un-American Activities. His anthology of poems *Manual of Piety* (first published in 1927) is highly recommended reading.

LUIS BUÑUEL.
Born 1900 in Calanda, Spain. Died 1983.
One of the great directors in cinema history, Buñuel joined the Surrealist Movement in Paris during the late 1920's. It was there he produced his early masterpieces Un Chien Andalou (1928) and L'Age d'or (1930), the latter of which caused a major scandal due to its savage assault on Christianity, the establishment and middle class morality. During the 1940's, Buñuel began work for the Museum of Modern Art in New York, but was ultimately fired because, in his words, "Salvador Dalí called me an atheist." After a decade of more commercial-oriented projects made in Mexico, Buñuel entered his greatest period of film making during the 1960's and 1970's. Among his masterpieces from this period are Viridiana (1961), The Exterminating Angel (1962), Belle de Jour (1967) and The Discreet Charm of the Bourgeoisie (1972). Buñuel's autobiography *My Last Sigh,* written shortly before his death, is highly recommended reading.

JOHN COLTRANE.
Born 1926 in Hamlet, North Carolina. Died 1967.
Coltrane, an innovative jazz musician and composer, first gained notoriety during the 1950's when he played saxophone opposite such musical giants as Charlie "Bird" Parker and Miles Davis. During the mid 1960's he began some of his most daring compositional experiments, often shattering many of the boundaries and confinements of traditional jazz music. Among his greatest recordings from this period are <u>Ascension</u> (1965), <u>Om</u> (1965), <u>Meditations</u> (1965) and <u>Interstellar Space</u> (1967).

PAUL ELUARD.
Born 1895 in Saint-Denis, France. Died 1952.
Eluard, a founder of Surrealism in 1920's Paris, quickly established himself as one of the movement's finest poets. In 1932, after his wife Gala's passionate affair with the artist Salvador Dalí, Eluard's marriage ended in divorce. His love for Gala, however, persisted, and he continued writing her painful letters of adoration throughout the remainder of his life.

KURT GERRON.
Born 1897 in Berlin, Germany. Died 1944.
An actor and cabaret performer in Germany during the 1920's, Gerron appeared in the original productions of Brecht's <u>Threepenny Opera</u> (1928) and <u>Happy End</u> (1929), as well as in the film <u>The Blue Angel</u> (1930) directed by Joseph von Sternberg and starring Emil Jannings. Mister Gerron was murdered in a concentration camp during World War II.

GUNTER GRASS.
Born 1927 in Danzig. Died 2015.
Grass was one of Germany's most celebrated contemporary writers, best known for his remarkable novel <u>The Tin Drum</u>.

EMIL JANNINGS.
Born 1884 in Rorschach, Switzerland. Died 1950.
One of the great actors in Europe during the 1920's, Jannings appeared in a large number of stage plays, as well as in several landmark films including F.W. Murnau's The Last Laugh (1924) and Joseph von Sternberg's The Blue Angel (1930). He was an enthusiastic supporter of the Nazi Party and often accepted roles in propaganda films produced by Josef Goebbels. In 1938 he received an award by Goebbels and was appointed as the head of *Tobis,* a Nazi production company. In 1941 he was honored as "Artist of the State". Jannings was forced into retirement in 1945 after Germany's defeat in the war.

KING CRIMSON.
A progressive rock band since the late 1960's, headed by guitarist Robert Fripp. Among their most notable recordings are Larks' Tongues in Aspic (1973) and Starless and Bible Black (1974). A box set of their live performances from 1973-1974 is now available.

D.H. LAWRENCE.
Born 1885 in Nottinghamshire. Died 1930.
An original and controversial English writer of the early 20th century, Lawrence produced a great variety of literary works including the novels Sons and Lovers, Women in Love and Lady Chatterly's Lover.

FEDERICO GARCIA LORCA.
Born 1899 in Fuente Vaqueros, Spain. Died 1936.
Lorca was a brilliant poet who also gained notoriety for his plays Blood Wedding and The House of Bernarda Alba. Perhaps his most memorable anthology of poems is Poet in New York, written while a student at Columbia University during the early 1930's. Lorca was murdered by Fascist supporters of Franco in 1936.

BIRGIT NILSSON.
Born 1918 in Sweden. Died 2005.
Among the great sopranos in music history, Nilsson's immortal voice had the power to cut through even the largest orchestra. Her recording of Wagner's *Tristan und Isolde* is highly recommended listening.

GUSTAVO OCTAVIO.
Born 1968 in Los Angeles, California.
An enigmatic performer who garnered praise for his remarkable portrayal of Moni in the original production of The Last of the Living Surrealists, Octavio left for New York in 1990 with dreams of exhibiting his experimental art work. Mysteriously, he disappeared and has not been heard from since.

OLIVER REED.
Born 1938 in Wimbledon, London. Died 1999.
Reed was a fine British actor who appeared in a great number of films including Oliver (1968), Women in Love (1970) and Tommy (1975).

JULIUS STREICHER.
Born 1885 in Fleinhausen, Germany. Died 1946.
Through his anti-Semitic newspaper *Der Sturmer,* and through his charismatic speeches at Nazi rallies, Streicher helped persuade the German public to hate Jews. During the 1920's he headed a Nuremberg branch of the Nazi Party and developed his close association with Adolf Hitler. Streicher was executed in 1946 for crimes committed against humanity.

LEON TROTSKY
Born 1879 in The Ukraine. Died 1940.
A Soviet political leader, a theoretician of Marxism, an outstanding writer and orator, and the chief organizer of the Red Army

during the Revolution, Trotsky was forced to leave Russia after Lenin's death and the rise of Stalin. He was murdered in Mexico in 1940 by one of Stalin's agents.

RICHARD WAGNER.
Born 1813 in Leipzig. Died 1883.
The greatest composer of German opera, and one of the crucial figures in 19th century music, Wagner is responsible for creating a new artistic form: *The Music Drama*. All of his important compositions are for the theater, including his masterpieces Tristan und Isolde and The Ring Cycle. An anti-Semite (though he was of Jewish ancestry), Wagner was praised the greatest composer in history by Adolf Hitler. His operas were often played in concentration camps while Jews were being gassed to death.

HUGO WOLF.
Born 1860 in Austria. Died 1903.
A composer best known for his lieder, Wolf spent the final years of his life in a private mental asylum.

Goldring – The First Generation

A Medium Length Play
(1989)

Goldring – The First Generation is the first in a trilogy of medium length plays that partly reflect the history of the 20th Century. It is dedicated to my friend Gustavo Jimenez.

Characters

The Goldring Family

Harry *a fan salesman*
Josaphene *his wife*
Joseph *his brother*
Little Harry *his son*
Four Daughters
Mrs. Melish *an adopted grandmother*
The Narrator *Little Harry as a grown man*

Additional Characters

The Accordion Player *also known as Jerry*
Eileen *The Accordion Player's wife*
Epstein & Dryer *a gallery owner and his advisor*
The Maid *also known as Marie*
J.P. Bower & Rolo *a business tycoon and his associate*
Donald, Gordy & Luis *friends of Harry*
Gilbert & Joey *classmates of Little Harry*
The Newsboy & The Revolutionary Boy
The Salesman *a street peddler*
The Master of Ceremonies *an employee of Begbick's nightclub*
The Cop & The Officer *public servants*
Moe *an innocent bystander*
Man 1 & Man 2
Three Crowd Members *Crowd Member 2 is also known as Jacob*

As well as...

Cops, prisoners, spectators, and children

Prologue

Ladies and gentlemen,
Tonight you're going to see a thing
Our playwright, Mister Bash, calls Goldring.
It's about a man - Harry's his name
who designed fans with a special aim.
He created images that reflected society
The lunacy of Man, the silly Church piety.
Some of you may say that Harry's an artist
Financially, though, he's far from the smartest
But let's not give too much away
Otherwise you may not want to stay for the play.
Josaphene is someone else you'll meet
She's slyer than a fox, but not very sweet.
And Little Harry, their devoted son
He's got plans of his own to be done.
In fact, Little Harry appears in a follow-up play
But that's something for another day.
Right now, for your enjoyment and contemplation
We're ready to perform **Goldring - The First Generation**.
You're encouraged to sit back and go with the flow.
As for us, farewell, and on with the show!

NARRATOR: It was a dark September day. Eight years before my birth. My father and his brother came to this town with an incredible passion for fans. The sun and the moon were out simultaneously and the air smelled vaguely of wet shit. Yet for my father, he had entered the promised land. This was a town of opportunity.

(HARRY and JOSEPH have entered, pulling wagons filled with electrical fans.)

HARRY: I can feel it, Joseph. People here care about art. They support growth and exploration. We should have no problems selling our fans.

JOSEPH: I feel the same way, Harry.

HARRY: This is the beginning of a new era for us. Soon we shall stain the minds of all men and women with images that will haunt each for the rest of his or her life.

JOSEPH: It is time to put the real world on trial.

HARRY: It is time for change. And we're just the men who can make it happen.

NARRATOR: My father and his brother were among the first fan salesmen to completely create their own fans. Within a month they had their own studio and were producing some of the most influential fans in Europe. My father gained particular recognition for his "Human Species" fan, which curiously resembled a giant asshole. It triggered a rash of riotous protests and caused what many consider the first major fan scandal in history.

(HARRY and JOSEPH have been removing their fans from the wagons and neatly placing them on a shelf and table. One of the fans resembles a giant asshole.)

MAN FROM OUTSIDE: *WE DEMAND YOU COME OUT, HAROLD GOLDRING! IF YOU DO NOT DESTROY THAT FAN, WE SHALL DESTROY YOUR SHOP!*

HARRY: It's the R.A.I.J. again, Joseph.

JOSEPH: *THE REVOLUTIONARY ARMY OF THE INFANT JESUS.*

HARRY: We mustn't let them intimidate us.

MAN FROM OUTSIDE: *YOU'VE GOT TEN SECONDS BEFORE WE OBLITERATE! NINE...EIGHT...*

(A bell rings as MRS. MELISH enters the shop. She is followed by three stray children.)

MRS. MELISH: Good morning, Mister Goldring.

HARRY: Good morning, Mrs. Melish.

CHILD: We've come to see the asshole fan.

MAN FROM OUTSIDE (simultaneous to the above exchange): SEVEN, SIX, FIVE, FOUR, THREE, TWO, ONE. *OBLITERATE!!!*

(Roars, bangs and crashes are heard.)

JOSEPH: They're smashing the building!

MRS. MELISH: I'd like to buy a fan for my daughter.

HARRY: Stand back, Mrs. Melish. We may need to retaliate.

JOSEPH: They've got a gun, Harry. I can see a boy with a gun.

HARRY: Take cover! Everyone take cover!

(A whistle is heard.)

MAN FROM OUTSIDE: *COPS!*

COP: *HOLT! IN THE NAME OF THE LAW!*

(The sounds of scampering feet are heard, followed by two loud gunshots.)

COP: *COME HERE! YOU LITTLE HOODLUM!*

(Two more shots are heard.)

COP: *GOTCHA!*

(A struggle is heard, then the COP enters, handcuffing a young REVOLUTIONARY BOY.)

COP: I got one, Mister Goldring. The others ran away.

REVOLUTIONARY BOY: *THIS MAN IS MEPHISTOPHELIAN! HE CREATES FOR THE DEVIL!*

COP: I'll try to get some reinforcement down here as soon as I can.

REVOLUTIONARY BOY: LOOK! (He points at the children,

who are viewing Harry's asshole fan.) *HE CORRUPTS THE MINDS OF OUR YOUTH! HE DESTROYS THE MORAL FIBER OF OUR PEOPLE!*

COP: Is this what all the commotion's about?

REVOLUTIONARY BOY: *IT IS OBSCENE! IT IS AGAINST THE WORD OF GOD!!!*

COP: I'm afraid I must agree.

HARRY: I spent a lot of time and effort on that fan. It is my personal expression of humanity.

COP: It is pornography, therefore it must be confiscated.

JOSEPH: But that fan goes up for auction in less than two hours.

COP: Not anymore it doesn't. AS OF NOW, THIS FAN IS OFFICIAL PROPERTY OF THE GOVERNMENT CENSOR!

NARRATOR: My father fought the censor in a court battle that lasted nearly fourteen months. In the end his fan remained banned, but his popularity grew to the status of cult hero. He was praised a model rebel by a group of insurgent intellectuals who immediately accepted him into their ranks. Influenced by his new friends, father created some of his most daring and unorthodox fans, constantly challenging the authority of the censor. His "Welcome to the World, Baby" fan depicted an infant, thrust from his mother's womb, landing in a bucket of glop-covered crucifixes. And his "Portrait of Galileo" presented a model of the astronomer forced at gun point by a priest to turn round and round and round.

(HARRY and JOSEPH have removed each of the above described fans and neatly placed them on a table.)

> By night my father and his brother would attend meetings among the intellectuals and discuss art, the possibility for change, the idiocy of religion, and the anti-bourgeoisie acts each would commit the following day. While some individuals were imprisoned for defacing public property, my father chose lighter crimes such as flipping off government officials, sending envelopes enclosed with blank pieces of paper through the mail, and going door to door and asking for himself.

(HARRY and JOSEPH wait outside a door.)

HARRY: Pardon me, but is there a Harry and Joseph Goldring here?

WOMAN: I'm sorry. I don't know anyone by those names.

NARRATOR: My father's life was completely absorbed by the intellectuals. Until one day he met a distraction. It was at the grocery store by a crate of medium-sized tangelos. Here my father met my mother. And after a moment of frozen eyes, their lives would never be the same again.

(HARRY and JOSAPHENE stand on the stage and stare at one another. The ACCORDION PLAYER accompanies the two with soft, romantic music. After a tender pause, HARRY removes from behind his back a small, red fan in the shape of a heart. JOSAPHENE is touched. She kisses HARRY on his cheek and takes the fan. After a pause, she offers Harry her hand. He takes it. And the two slowly walk upstage and disappear into the darkness. The ACCORDION PLAYER continues his music for about ten seconds, then he stops. *Pause.* He walks off the stage. *Silence.*)

NARRATOR: That night my father pressed his flesh inside my mother and they became one. Nine months later their first offspring was born.

(The cries of JOSAPHENE in labor are heard, as HARRY paces the stage, puffing a cigarette.)

JOSAPHENE: UNNMMM! UNNMMMMMMM!
UNNNNMMMMMMMMMM!
UNNNNNNNMMMMMMMMMMM!!!
UNNNNNNNMMMMMMMMMM!!!
UNNNNNNNMMMMMMMMMMM!!!!!!
UNNMMMMMMMMMMMMMMMMMMMMMM
MMMMMMMMMMMMM!!!!!!!!!!!!!!!!!!!!!!!!!!!!!!!!!!!!

DOCTOR: Congratulations, Mister Goldring.

HARRY: Is it a boy or a girl?

DOCTOR: It's four girls. Your wife's just had quadruplets.

(The heads of four baby girls pop up and fill the theatre with loud, obnoxious cries.)

DAUGHTERS:
WAAAAAAAAAAAAA!! WAAAAAAAAAAAAA!!
WAAAAAAAAAAAAA!! WAAAAAAAAAAAAA!!

NARRATOR (shouting so he can be heard):

DESPITE THE DISTRACTION,	*WAAAAAAAA!*
MY FATHER'S FANS OBTAINED	*WAAAAAAAA!*
A NEW HEIGHT IN	*WAAAAAAAA!*
CREATIVITY DURING THE	*WAAAAAAAA!*
NEXT FIVE MONTHS. HIS	*WAAAAAAAA!*
BUSINESS BOOMED AND HIS	*WAAAAAAAA!*

SEXUAL DRIVE PEAKED AS	*WAAAAAAAA!*
HE HUMPED MY MOTHER	*WAAAAAAAA!*
NEARLY EVERY NIGHT.	*WAAAAAAAA!*

(A bed is rolled upon the stage. In it, HARRY and JOSAPHENE fuck beneath the covers.)

JOSAPHENE: UHH. UHH. UHH.	*WAAAAAAAA!*
AHHHHHH. AHHHHHHHH.	*WAAAAAAAA!*
UHHHHHHHHHHH.	*WAAAAAAAA!*
UHHHHHHHHHHHHHH.	*WAAAAAAAA!*
OHHHHHHHHHH.	*WAAAAAAAA!*
OHHHHHHHHHHHHHH.	*WAAAAAAAA!*
UHHHHHHHHHHHHH.	*WAAAAAAAA!*
UHHHHHHHHHHHH.	*WAAAAAAAA!*
oh. oh. Ah. Ah. uhhhhhhhhhh.	*WAAAAAAAA!*
uhhhhhhhhh. uhhhhhhhhhh.	*WAAAAAAAA!*
UHHHHHHHHHHHHHH.	*WAAAAAAAA!*
UHHHHHHHHHHHHHHHH!	*WAAAAAAAA!*
UHHHHHHHHHHHHHHHH-	*WAAAAAAAA!*
HHHHHHHHHHHHHHHHH-	*WAAAAAAAA!*
HHHHHHHHHHHHHHHHH-	*WAAAAAAAA!*
HHHHHHHHHHHHHHHH!!!!!!	*WAAAAAAAA!*
!!!	

(*Quiet.*)

NARRATOR: And thus I was conceived.

BLACKOUT.

SALESMAN: Step right up! Step right up, folks! I got "Welcome to the World, Baby" T shirts here. Two for the price of one! I got some mugs I got some jugs I got some little things you shake up at Christmas time and watch the snow fall. I even got this authentic, non-conformist baby doll who chants eight different slogans of societal anarchy.

BABY DOLL: *Fuck the bourgeoisie! Fuck the bourgeoisie!*

SALESMAN: Don't crowd. There's enough for all. And remember, if you don't buy "Goldring" products, you're missing out on what everyone's talking about!

PHOTOGRAPHER: Hold it!

(HARRY poses for a photograph with two attractive women who wear bikinis that feature round electrical fans for breast covers. An old fashioned camera flash, or mini explosion, occurs.)

PHOTOGRAPHER: Okay. Let's bring on those live lobsters!

NARRATOR: In January of the following year, my father's business was named one of the top grossing corporations in the nation. My sisters began wearing exotic chimpanzee furs and my mother hired an assortment of maids, butlers and legal consultants. By mid February our home had been transformed into a castle and our lives were lived like popes. My father's popularity was challenging stardom.

(JOSAPHENE appears, discussing business matters with a gallery owner and his advisor.)

JOSAPHENE: You understand I am fully responsible for all of Mister Goldring's financial affairs.

EPSTEIN: I do. My partner and I have come to offer a large sum of money in exchange for two exhibits by your husband. Before you answer, I'd like to inform you that our gallery is among the most influential repositories in the Eastern Hemisphere. We admire your husband's work, Mrs. Goldring. He has something to say...and he should be heard. One month in our gallery and his fans could be elevated from a temporary fad to a permanent innovation.

(*Pause.*)

JOSAPHENE: You mentioned a large sum of money. Could you be more specific?

EPSTEIN: Of course.

(EPSTEIN writes the amount on a small piece of paper and hands it to JOSAPHENE.)

JOSAPHENE (examines the paper): Hm. (*Pause.*) Please excuse me.

(JOSAPHENE walks across the room, removes a small bell and rings it. A young MAID immediately enters.)

MAID: Yes madam.

JOSAPHENE: I'll be ready for lunch soon. Here. Take this.

(She hands the MAID Epstein's paper.)

MAID: Yes madam.

(The MAID exits.)

JOSAPHENE: Tell me, gentlemen. Do you enjoy steak?

EPSTEIN: Yes.

DRYER: Not when it's pink. But when well done, certainly. We all need our protein.

JOSAPHENE: Good. Because I enjoy steak, too. It's sort of a regular around here. Unfortunately, steaks are rather expensive these days. They cost a pretty penny. Therefore, my husband and I need to earn as many pretty pennies as possible. The more pretty pennies, the more steak. Do you follow?
(She removes a piece of paper and begins writing.) Mister Goldring has been offered this amount of money to design wallpaper for a major radio star's apartment house. Can you match it? (She hands the paper to EPSTEIN.)

EPSTEIN (examines the paper): I'm afraid that's a bit out of our price range.

DRYER: I can assure you, though, that our gallery would be far more beneficial for Mister Goldring's career than...

JOSAPHENE: If you can not pay the required fee then I'd say you have some gall in coming here. (She suddenly kicks EPSTEIN hard in his ass.)

EPSTEIN: OUCH!

JOSAPHENE: Now dismiss yourselves before I report both of you to the authorities for impersonating men!

DRYER: Mrs. Goldring!

JOSAPHENE: I said dismiss yourselves. Now!

(She boots DRYER.)

DRYER: Ohhhh!

EPSTEIN: You're only hurting yourself.

(EPSTEIN and DRYER exit. After a pause, the MAID enters carrying a plate of raw meat.)

MAID: Your steak, madam.

(The MAID places the plate on a table, then exits. JOSAPHENE eyes the meat, slowly walks toward it, then begins to savagely devour it. Grunts and growls and other animalistic sounds are heard as she does so.)

(*Meanwhile*, opposite stage, HARRY and JOSEPH appear.)

HARRY: Its happening, Joseph. Our images are staining the minds of men and women everywhere. Do you know yesterday morning an infant had my "Galileo" fan imprinted upon his rattle?

JOSEPH: It's marvelous, Harry. There is one problem that does disturb me, however.

HARRY: Disturb you?

JOSEPH: Yes. I feel we're devoting too much focus on publicity and not enough on fans. Why, between photographic sessions and luncheons, it's been nearly nine months since either one of us has had time to complete a fan.

HARRY: You're absolutely right. Josaphene's master scheme to change life has succeeded as planned. Yet fans must always remain our number one loyalty.

JOSEPH: I suggest we design a new fan line immediately. It is our duty as dedicated salesmen.

HARRY: I shall suggest your suggestion to Josaphene the moment I get home.

NARRATOR: It was one hour later, at a bus stop near Grand Avenue, that my mother's master scheme continued to blossom. It captured an innocent bystander named Moe, whose baby daughter Flo had been suffering from severe diaper rash.

(FLO is heard crying from within her baby carriage. MOE attempts to comfort her.)

MOE: There there, Flo. Don't cry. See what daddy's bought you? A genuine "Harold Goldring" doll. Shall we hear what it has to say? (He pulls the doll's cord.)

BABY DOLL: *Fuck the bourgeoisie! Fuck the bourgeoisie!*

(A COP suddenly appears and conks MOE on the head. MOE falls to the ground, unconscious, accompanied by birdie sounds.)

COP: I'm afraid you're under arrest for possession of obscene merchandise. As of yesterday, this doll was declared banned by the government censor. Take him away, boys.

(A group of police officers drags MOE offstage; but *first* they pick his pocket. The baby carriage remains, with Flo crying from within. Her cries continue throughout the following scene.

Meanwhile, JOSAPHENE has observed this event through binoculars from her window.)

JOSAPHENE: Splendid. Splendid. My master scheme is blossoming as planned. By tomorrow morning Harold Goldring's non-conformist doll shall cause a greater scandal than his earth shattering "Human Species" fan. (She calls for an assistant.) JILES! Report our story to the Daily News at once. And here - spread these lies to the tabloids. We can use all the publicity we can get.

JILES: Right, Mrs. G.

(JILES takes a humongous stack of papers - *the lies* - from JOSAPHENE and exits.)

JOSAPHENE (picks up the phone):
Spencer...Josaphene...Fine...
I'll need your troop of photographers by morning...Yes, things are going well... What?... I couldn't hear you, Spencer, speak up. Just a moment, Spencer.
(She calls for the MAID.) MARIE! MARIE!

MAID: Yes madam.

JOSAPHENE: **SHUT THAT KID UP!**

MAID: Yes madam.

(The MAID exits, then reappears outside by Flo's baby carriage. She lifts the baby up, then, displaying great athletic ability, punt kicks the infant offstage.)

JOSAPHENE: Sorry, Spencer...Of course...I'll tell you what I say...Yes. That's what I say. Before one can recite the words "Shit On Rye" my husband's doll will be on every front page this nation has to offer. You heard me, Spencer. Shit...On...

(Enter a NEWSBOY.)

NEWSBOY: EXTRA! EXTRA! READ ALL ABOUT IT! GOLDRING DOLL CAUSES MAJOR SCANDAL. R.A.I.J. RIOT OUTSIDE TOY STORE LEADS TO PROHIBITION OF DOLL AS CHILDREN REBEL IN THE STREETS. EXTRA!

(Two men pass by reading the paper.)

FIRST MAN: Hm. It says here on page forty-seven in tiny print that an infant was discovered abandoned yesterday. Her father was executed for neglect.

SECOND MAN: It says here on page seventy-nine that another woman was raped and murdered. That makes eleven this week.

FIRST MAN: Oh well. That's life in the big city.

NARRATOR: After several hours of serious contemplation, my father returned home to announce his latest conclusion to Josaphene. Previously that night, he and Joseph had concluded that beginning promptly all current commitments would be put on hold and one hundred percent of their time would be devoted to the design and development of fans. My mother listened attentively before responding.

JOSAPHENE: ***DON'T EVER UTTER SUCH STUPIDITY AGAIN!*** I am in charge of all financial affairs here, Harry. Do you trust my judgment?

HARRY: Of course.

JOSAPHENE: *THEN DON'T COME TO CONCLUSIONS ANYMORE!*

HARRY: I'm only doing what I feel is my responsibility as an artist. I've got some say so around here, too, you know. I'm the one who does the creating.

JOSAPHENE: If you care about your creations *changing life* you'll allow me to continue my master scheme! Is that what you care about, Harry?

(*Pause.*)

HARRY: Well...yes.

JOSAPHENE: Then stop your babbling and get ready.

HARRY: Get ready? For what?

JOSAPHENE: Your first singing lesson. You're going to cut an album, Harry. And it's going to cause a greater scandal than all of your previous creations put together!

MUSIC!

MASTER OF CEREMONIES: Ladies and gentlemen. Boys and girls. It brings me great pleasure to introduce tonight's musical guest here at Begbick's. Put your hands together for an artist who is currently the talk of the town. He's the coolest cat and the meanest rat.
The one and only fan man himself –
HAROLD GOLDRING!

HARRY (sings): My name is Harold Goldring
and my life is selling fans.
I spread the truth where truth's opposed,
my stuff is always banned.
The Christians say I'm wicked,
the Jews and gays are too,
It's up to us to change the world
It's up to me and you
It's up to me and you
It's up to me and you
HEY!

The world's in need of changing,
it sucks the way it is.
There's too much crime and too much slime
and too much plop plop fizz.
The rich control the cities,
the poor eat shit for lunch,
the bourgeoisie's stupidity
It's time to say TOO MUCH!
It's time to say TOO MUCH!
It's time to say TOO MUCH!
HEY!

The rich man goes for cat scans
at least two times a week.
They find his lump and cut it out
and send him home to sleep.
The poor man goes for cancer
once it's far too late,
They sit him down to fill out forms
and say, "don't hesitate."
The doctor bursts from nowhere
and kicks him out the door.

He says, "sorry," "you' won't see me,"
"Good day, fuck you, you're poor!"
"Good day, fuck you, you're poor!"
"Good day, fuck you, you're poor!"
HEY!

(Members of the R.A.I.J. are becoming rowdy. They boo and hiss and toss pieces of rotten fruit on stage. Suddenly, a full riot has broken out. Cops burst upon the scene and begin beating HARRY.)

(During the commotion, J.P. BOWER, a business tycoon, appears down stage. He speaks with an associate.)

J.P. BOWER: There's nothing more pleasant than watching the common people beat one another to a pulp.

ROLO: Do you think they even have a clue what's about to happen?

J.P. BOWER: Of course not. They're common.
(*Brief Pause.*) Come on. I have a meeting with my financial advisor in ten minutes.

(J.P. BOWER and ROLO exit. The riot continues for several seconds.)

BLACKOUT.

(*Quiet*, then lights slowly rise on JOSAPHENE, who is meeting with JOSEPH.)

JOSAPHENE: It's not going to happen. I am in charge here, Joseph. I make the decisions.

JOSEPH: I'm only telling you what he told me. And frankly, I agree with him one hundred percent.

JOSAPHENE: I didn't ask for your opinion. Harry's tour shall continue as planned. Any cancellation or shift of focus to fan development is definitely out of the question.

(HARRY staggers into the room, out of breath, bruised, and wearing bandages.)

HARRY: I'm afraid that's not correct!

JOSAPHENE (startled): Harry.

HARRY: I'm going to put my foot down, Josaphene. And this time it's for real. Beginning today, my absolute focus will return to the design and construction of fans.

JOSAPHENE: Darling. You don't mean that.

HARRY: Joseph. Prepare to begin research on police corruption. I've got at least nine ideas stewing inside my noodle.

JOSEPH: Right.

HARRY: And here. (He hands a fan blueprint to JOSAPHENE.) Initiate a publicity campaign for this. I feel it could have staining potential.

JOSAPHENE: No. You're not qualified to make these decisions, Harry. I'm the one in charge here.

HARRY: Then as my advisor maybe you should support me on what I'm trying to do.

JOSAPHENE: I'll support you on what needs to be done. Do you see this? (She removes a newspaper.) The economy is spiraling downhill. By Christmas a full depression will devastate every home in the working class.

HARRY: That's all the more reason for us to focus on fans.

JOSAPHENE: People can't afford fans!
In times of hardship, Harry, people need to escape. Your musical performances are one way of helping them do so.

HARRY: It's not about helping people escape, Josaphene. Now come on. There's work to be done.

JOSAPHENE: I forbid you to continue!
(HARRY exits.)
Harry!
HARRY!
(She rushes to the telephone.)
Spencer...Josaphene...I'm afraid there's trouble... You heard me, Spencer.
Shit...On...

(Enter a Newsboy.)

NEWSBOY: EXTRA! EXTRA! READ ALL ABOUT IT! DEPRESSION HITS CITY! THOUSANDS UNEMPLOYED! EXTRA!

MAN 1 (speaks directly to the audience):
Ladies and gentlemen. There is a problem in our society. As of today, nearly eight of every ten men are unemployed. Crime is rampant in the streets. And cannibalism is on the rise. Yesterday morning my mother was eaten by a group of recently fired auto workers! Now I can understand you're cold and hungry. I can understand you're homeless

and your families and friends are dying from murder and disease. I can even understand you're angry and frustrated and feel like shoving your fist down someone's fucking throat. But eating one another is not the answer. We are not savages here! We are human beings! We have the power to think and rationalize thoughts! It is in difficult times like these that we must come together. We must form a bond and remain together like glops of *Elmer's Glue.* Don't you see. We are not savages! We must help each other. We are *human beings!*
(A hungry auto worker bites into the flesh of MAN 1.)
Ahhhhhhhhhhhh!!!! WE MUSTN'T RESORT TO CANNIBALISM! WE MUST TRY TO BE FRIENDS! WE ARE HUMAN BEINGS! WE ARE **HUMAN BEINGS!!!!!**

(A second auto worker begins to eat MAN 1.)

MAN 2 (speaks directly to the audience, simultaneous to MAN 1, beginning at the sentence "Now I can understand..."): Ladies and Gentlemen. Do you get annoyed when your favorite radio shows are distracted due to the amount of heat in your home? Are you women tired of having your husband's sweat stain the fabric of your best antique chairs? Do you men become irritated by chafed legs caused by moisture within your crotch due to perspiration-inducing heat? Well the time has come to toss away those rickety old fans and enter the new age of modern comfort. The time has come...*for central air conditioning!* In two short weeks and a mere fifteen thousand dollars, we can install one of these babies in your home. The motor produces air and the ducts relay that air throughout your entire quarters. Now the day can seem like night and you can relax in your snobby little castles just like the rich were made to act. Who wants one of these babies?

(Three or four men and women wearing tuxedos and fancy evening gowns rush to buy their central air-conditioning units.)

MEN AND WOMEN: *I want one! I'll take one! Let me have one!*

(*Meanwhile*, on the other side of the stage –)

MAN 1: **AHHHHHHHHHHHHHHHHHHHHHHHH!!!!!**

(MAN 1 is eaten. Blood spills from his body and blood drips from the mouths of the two hungry auto workers.)

MAN 1 (a final gasp): Help.

(The men and women in tuxedos and fancy evening gowns continue their pursuit for happiness and the perfect air-conditioning.)

BLACKOUT.

(A muffled voice is heard from a radio.)

VOICE: It is now more than ever we must have strength. Times of instability are more susceptible to change, therefore, no matter how bleak things may appear to be, we must continue onward and fight.

(*Silence*, then lights up on Harry's fan shop. HARRY and JOSEPH are removing their fans from the shelf and table and neatly placing them, once again, in the wagons. They are preparing to leave. A bell rings as MRS. MELISH enters the shop.)

JOSEPH: Good morning, Mrs. Melish. I'm afraid our business is no longer here. But don't fret, beginning next week we shall reopen shop at Harry's residence.

MRS. MELISH: I'm sorry, Mister Goldring, but I've no money for fans. You see my husband's been murdered and my children have disappeared. I can't afford to pay my rent and was hoping I could stay here for a day or two.

HARRY: Your husband murdered?! How?!

MRS. MELISH: It seems a stray bullet entered the window and struck him in his head. I tried to get help, but when I returned...(She begins crying.)...*He had been eaten!*

HARRY: My gosh. How horrible.

MRS. MELISH: *I don't know what I'm going to do!*

HARRY: Don't cry, Mrs. Melish. You've been a good and faithful customer. You can come home with me. My wife and five children won't mind.

MRS. MELISH: Thank you, Mister Goldring. You're a kind man. (She loudly blows her nose into a handkerchief.)

NARRATOR: I was seven years old when Mrs. Melish came to live with us. Between mass unemployment and the Rich's obsession for central air-conditioning, my father's fan business hit rock bottom. My mother often encouraged him to change occupations in order to reap greater financial benefits.

JOSAPHENE: YOU'RE A BUM! WHY DON'T YA DO WHAT I SAY FOR CRISSAKE!

HARRY: I put food on the table.

JOSAPHENE: YOU DON'T PUT NOTHIN' ON THAT TABLE!

HARRY: I don't put nothin' on that table?

JOSAPHENE: YOU DON'T PUT NOTHIN' ON THAT TABLE!

HARRY: ***I DON'T PUT NOTHIN' ON THAT TABLE?!***

JOSAPHENE: Look at you.

HARRY: WHAT?!

JOSAPHENE: Look at you!

HARRY: *WHAT?!*

JOSAPHENE: ***LOOK AT YOU!!***

(*Pause.*)

JOSAPHENE: I'm tired of this, Harry. I'm tired of you and these fans. You don't even sleep with me anymore. You don't care if your kids eat shit for lunch. All you care about are these goddamn fans. Well this is what I think about your fans, Harry. **This is what I think about your fans!** (She begins smashing one of his fans.) **Fuck your fans!** Do you hear me? **Fuck your fans! FUCK YOUR FANS! *FUCK YOUR FANS!!***

(Throughout the course of the play, cops periodically roam in the background, listening in on other people's conversations. They hold glasses up to walls and peek through keyholes. One of these cops has just burst upon the stage, pointing a gun at JOSAPHENE.)

COP: Hold it right there! I'm afraid you're in violation of the language obscenity law. You'll have to come with me.

(The COP begins handcuffing JOSAPHENE.)

JOSAPHENE: What are you doing?

COP: Sentence is fourteen hours. You can pick her up in the morning, mac.

JOSAPHENE: Harry! Do something!

HARRY: Whata ya want me to do?

JOSAPHENE: Hit him!

HARRY: He's got a gun.

JOSAPHENE: Well don't just stand there!

(The COP escorts JOSAPHENE offstage.)

JOSAPHENE: Harry! Harry!

HARRY: I'll see you in the morning.

JOSAPHENE: Harry! Do something!
HARRRRRYYYYYYYY!!!!!!!!!!

(JOSAPHENE and the COP exit, as LITTLE HARRY, a seven year old boy enters.)

LITTLE HARRY: Daddy. Where is mommy going with that cop?

HARRY: Away, son. Away. (*Pause*.) You understand me, don't you? What I do with fans is purely a form of my own expression. I mean I have a need to express myself.
(He removes a fan.) Come here. I want you to touch this. Put your hand here.
(The child does so.) Do you feel it? (*Brief pause*.) This is a fan, son. This is an object of immense beauty. By simply using our fingers we are capable of transforming a dead flower into life. (He turns on the fan.) Do you see it? Can you sense its truth?
(*Pause*.)
Our responsibility as human beings is to spread this truth, even if it is everywhere opposed.
Your uncle Joseph and I are not good salesmen. We can create, but we cannot sell. Therefore, we must find someone who is willing to help us.
(*Pause*.)
Do you feel it?
(*Pause*.)
You don't feel it, do you?
(*Pause*.)
You don't feel it.

(*Quiet*.)

NARRATOR: On Friday morning my father returned home with my mother and began an argument that lasted nearly ten hours. At nine P.M. father tossed an ashtray across the room and began packing his genuine goatskin suitcase.

JOSAPHENE: Go ahead. Leave. YOU SON OF A BITCH!!

NARRATOR: Eight minutes later, mother gathered my sisters and me for an urgent family meeting.

JOSAPHENE: Your father has left the family, children. It's not going to be easy, but we must continue on without him. Little Harry. From now on you're the man of this house. I want you to behave yourself. And Mrs. Melish. You can watch the children while I'm at work.

LITTLE HARRY: Mommy. Where is daddy?

JOSAPHENE: You mustn't think about him anymore. All of you. From now on it's only us. The seven of us are a family. Everything's going to be okay.

(Lights fade. After a pause, the ACCORDION PLAYER and his wife appear, performing music on a street. The Accordion Player's clothes are different from those worn in previous scenes. He is now clearly homeless.)

ACCORDION PLAYER (sings):
    It wasn't too long ago I was at *Begbick's*
    playing for sold out crowds.
    My name's Jerry and my wife's Eileen
    and my sons were Pete and McClowd.
    But now I'm here, out in the heat
    My bed is here, out in the street
    My wife's a slut
    My life's a rut
    And my bones are aching out loud.

    If you take a sniff you can smell a whiff
    of my children's flesh in the air.
    They were eaten by men
    and some old ladies too

who claimed that their cupboards were bare.
So now I'm here, a childless pop
My friends are here, harassed by the cops
They say today
We'll be okay
'Cause God upstairs really cares.

EILEEN AND JERRY (singing together):
He cares, He cares
That's why we're so happy.
He cares, He cares
Oh yes we're so happy.

JERRY:
Just take a look around you and see
It's obvious He cares.

EILEEN AND JERRY:
He cares, He cares
That's why we're so happy.
He cares, He cares
Oh yes we're so happy.

JERRY:
Just take a look around you and see
It's obvious He cares.
It's obvious He's there.

(LITTLE HARRY and his four sisters enter.)

EILEEN: Good morning, children. Off to school?

LITTLE HARRY: Yes, Mrs. Prostitute. I'm sorry I can't spare any change today. Mother said our family has landed upon hard times.

JERRY: Don't worry, son. God upstairs really does care. He won't let us suffer.

LITTLE HARRY: I hope not. In any case, if I ever do earn money, I'll certainly contribute some to you, Mister Accordion Player. The world is always in need of fine music.

JERRY: You're a smart boy. Now on your way. You mustn't be late for school.

EILEEN: And be sure to watch both ways. The cannibals might try to eat you the same way they did our poor sons Pete and McClowd.

LITTLE HARRY: Mother prepared us for that, Mrs. Prostitute. I'm holding some mace.

SISTERS: And we brought our guns.

(The sisters display their weapons.)

EILEEN: So long, children.

LITTLE HARRY: So long. I'll see you after school.

(LITTLE HARRY and his sisters exit.)

EILEEN: Do you really think they'll be okay?

JERRY: I don't know. Perhaps we should pray for their safety: Dear God. May our little friends remain safe and sound. (*Pause.*) He cares you know. (*Pause.*)
Come on. Let's find another corner.

(JERRY and EILEEN exit. After a pause, LITTLE HARRY

re-enters and speaks directly to the audience.)

LITTLE HARRY: It is at this point our story takes a strange and unusual turn. You see, my father is nowhere to be found and I, Harry Jr., must aid my mother in supporting our family. The question is...how to do so? I considered this problem for some days. Then, on Thursday afternoon, the answer came to me like a lead pipe across my forehead.

(A lead pipe falls from above and crashes onto the floor.)

THE VOICE OF HARRY SENIOR: Your uncle Joseph and I are not good salesmen. We can create, but we cannot sell. Therefore, we must find someone who is willing to help us.

LITTLE HARRY: The answer: I SHALL SELL.

(A school bell rings.)

THE VOICE OF A FEMALE TEACHER: Okay, children. Time for lunch.

(The sounds of scampering feet are heard.)

FEMALE TEACHER: Walk. Don't run. Goddamnit! I said walk!

(JOEY and GILBERT, two eight year old children, enter the stage.)

JOEY (reading a paper): It says here tuna fish sandwiches are down to two cents.

GILBERT: I sure am glad my mother made peanut butter and jelly.

LITTLE HARRY: Did you say your mother made peanut butter and jelly?

JOEY: P and J sandwiches hold tight at four dimes.

LITTLE HARRY: Don't read that garbage, Joey. (He tears away the paper and tosses it aside.) They don't know what they're printing. Come here and I'll show you a real bargain.

GILBERT: You got brownies, Harry?

LITTLE HARRY: More than that. (He removes a sandwich from a brown paper bag.) Feast your eyes on this, boys.

GILBERT (after a pause): What is it?

LITTLE HARRY: Tuna. Now I know you're thinking it's only two cents. And maybe you're right. But then again, maybe you're not. The fact is it's all relevant to how you look at things. Did I ever tell you about my uncle Robert?

JOEY: I...

LITTLE HARRY: My uncle Robert was a sailor. Kind of like that guy in your comic book.

GILBERT: You mean the one with the wooden leg and hook arm?

LITTLE HARRY: Yeah. That's him.

JOEY: The one with the patch over his eye?

LITTLE HARRY: Yeah.

JOEY: He was great.

GILBERT: Yeahhhhh.

LITTLE HARRY: So my uncle Robert is just like that. And he goes sailing out at sea for months or sometimes even years.

GILBERT: Wow.

LITTLE HARRY: And he's out there fishing, right? He's out there fishing, hunting for food. Catches an eight hundred pound tuna.

JOEY: Eight hundred pounds?!

LITTLE HARRY: And he's reeling it in. He's fighting it for nine hours.

GILBERT: Like that hunter who fought that buffalo.

LITTLE HARRY: Exactly. And he's reeling it in. And do you know what happens?

GILBERT AND JOEY: What?

(*Brief pause.*)

LITTLE HARRY: He kills it.
    Now I ask you, Gilbert. What is more valuable? A living animal who lost his life to satisfy your eating pleasure? Or a peanut tossed around with some smashed berries? (*Pause.*)
    I'm willing to trade this tuna sandwich for your P and J simply because my uncle Robert has more than a plentiful

supply of fish.

GILBERT: How do I know the sandwich is good?

LITTLE HARRY: Oh it's good, Gilbert. It is good.

(*Brief pause.*)

GILBERT: I'll take it.

LITTLE HARRY: You made the right choice.

(The two boys exchange sandwiches. GILBERT begins eating his, as he and JOEY exit. After a pause, LITTLE HARRY walks to an imaginary booth and says -)

LITTLE HARRY: I'd like to exchange this peanut butter and jelly sandwich for four dimes.

THE VOICE OF HARRY SENIOR: *NO!* There is no possible way one can create something from nothing.

(Focus shifts opposite stage, where HARRY and JOSEPH appear, discussing religion with a group of intellectuals.)

GORDY: That's what it says in the Bible. In the beginning there was absolute *nothingness.* From this God created Earth.

DONALD: Maybe we should end on that note, gentlemen. It's getting late.

LUIS: But I haven't told my joke about St. Simeon, who plopped himself atop this giant column in the middle of the desert...

DONALD: Save it for another discussion, Luis. I really must be going.

(He puts on his coat and hat.)

I'm afraid this shall be our final evening together, Harry. I'm deeply sorry, but I must collect my rent.

HARRY: Don't apologize, Donald. You've been a good and faithful friend. I thought a fan shop could succeed here. I guess I was wrong. I thank you for letting us try for as long as we did.

DONALD: I wish you all the best.

HARRY: You, too. Good-bye. (They shake hands.)

(DONALD, GORDY and LUIS exit. *Pause.*)

JOSEPH: What should we do now?

HARRY: It's time to go home, Joseph.

NARRATOR: My father returned home four months after he left. He sat on a stool for twelve hours, remaining completely still and silent. At six a.m. he slowly approached my mother.

HARRY: You were right, Josaphene. I admit defeat. Tomorrow morning I'll search for employment other than my fans.

NARRATOR: *MEANWHILE*, around the corner at Carlile square, a group of anxious laborers crowded the boulevard, shouting cries of joyous relief.

(A crowd gathers.)

CROWD MEMBER 1: What's going on?

CROWD MEMBER 2: Didn't you hear? The government has subsidized ninety central air-conditioning factories to be run by J.P. Bower. There's going to be jobs again!

CROWD MEMBER 1: *Hooray for J.P. Bower!*

OTHER CROWD MEMBERS: **HOORAY!!!**

HARRY (*opposite stage*): This is ridiculous. I'm not going to design pieces for central air-conditioning units.

JOSAPHENE: You said you were going to find employment. Well, that's what's out there, Harry. Now stop acting so damn proud and get your coat on. We're going to Carlile Square.

CROWD MEMBER 1: No longer will I go hungry.

CROWD MEMBER 3: The pay is small, but it's better than nothing. Maybe now I'll be able to afford my rent.

CROWD MEMBER 2: Get in line. They're handing out applications.

CROWD MEMBER 3: I was here first.

CROWD MEMBER 1: Screw you!

CROWD MEMBER 3: **Out of my way!**

(Enter HARRY and his family, including JOSEPH and MRS. MELISH, to Carlile square.)

HARRY: I never thought I'd see this day, Joseph. Life can certainly be a ballbuster.

LITTLE HARRY (to one of the crowd members): Hey, mister. Wanna buy a pen?

CROWD MEMBER 2: Don't bother me, kid.

LITTLE HARRY: It's made of genuine plastic. And look. When you turn it sideways you can see the breasts of a beautiful woman.

CROWD MEMBER 2 (interested): Hm. (He changes his mind.) Sorry. I can't afford it.

LITTLE HARRY: It's only nine cents. What is your name?

CROWD MEMBER 2: Jacob.

LITTLE HARRY: May I call you Jake?

CROWD MEMBER 2: I...

LITTLE HARRY: The world is full of opportunity, Jake. Sometimes, you need to snatch it when it bites you from behind. Do you see this? This is not an ordinary pen, my friend. This is an *opportunity* for you to sign that application with an instrument far superior to anyone else's. Do you believe in fate?

CROWD MEMBER 2: I'm not sure.

LITTLE HARRY: Fate has brought me here to change your life, Jake. The question is - Are you willing to accept that now is the time? I want you to say yes.

CROWD MEMBER 2: Yes?

LITTLE HARRY: You made the right choice. (He grabs some money from CROWD MEMBER 2 and hands him the pen.)

HARRY: Joseph. Did you see that?!

JOSEPH: Little Harry. He can sell.

HARRY: Son. Where did you learn this?

LITTLE HARRY: It came to me one day at school.

JOSAPHENE: It's obviously in his genes from *my* side of the family.

HARRY: It doesn't matter whose side of the family they're from. The point is our son is gifted. This could be the answer to our problem!

JOSAPHENE: What are you talking about?

HARRY: Little Harry. Your uncle Joseph and I need a good salesman to reopen our fan shop.

JOSAPHENE: I thought we just ended that?!

HARRY: If Harry is gifted, then maybe his sisters are, too. We could get them tested. The entire family could return to fans again!

JOSAPHENE: ***ENOUGH!*** I am now in charge of Little Harry's career. I refuse to let you corrupt him with that self-indulgent garbage.

HARRY: I'll corrupt him with whatever I want to!

LITTLE HARRY: Mom's right, dad. Fans are a part of the past. Central air-conditioning is where the money's at. I say we go in that direction.

HARRY (deeply hurt): Little Harry.

LITTLE HARRY: I can sell, you'll create, and mom can be in charge of publicity. It's a winning combination.

HARRY: Son. Fans are important. You can't just ignore your responsibility.

JOSAPHENE: Lighten up, Harry. It's time to do something smart for once in your life. Now let's get going. I'm suddenly getting ideas that will even put J.P. Bower in his place.

(The Goldring family, aside from HARRY and JOSEPH, begin to exit. LITTLE HARRY stops and comments to a man handing out applications.)

LITTLE HARRY: Shove that application in your ear, mister. The Goldrings are going into the central air-conditioning business!

(LITTLE HARRY continues on his way.)

(*Pause.*)

JOSEPH (to Harry): You going?

(*Silence*, then, suddenly, HARRY rushes to his son and begins smacking him across the head. A whistle is heard, as two cops enter. HARRY is conked from behind, accompanied by birdie sounds.)

BLACKOUT.

NARRATOR: My father entered the Boneyard County Jail on April 9th at eight P.M. His sentence for child abuse was life imprisonment or seven months designing propaganda posters for the government. He chose the former and was subsequently placed in a high security artist ward. On May 14 mother began holding auditions for potential replacements as family designer. The process was more difficult than first anticipated, so my sister Irma was enrolled at the Acme Institute of Arts and Air-conditioning.

HARRY: They must be hallucinating. If they believe a lifetime of creativity can be replaced by one year at some second rate art school, they're sadly mistaken.

COP: *GET IN LINE AND SOUND OFF!*

(HARRY and other members from the artist ward form a line and begin marching in a circle. Each prisoner wears a sign around his neck that reads "rebellious." The group is held at gun point by two cops.)

PRISONERS: *ONE. TWO. THREE. FOUR. ONE. TWO. THREE. FOUR.*

(The prisoners continue sounding off, as a young man speaks to HARRY.)

KYLE: Are you really Harold Goldring? *The* Harold Goldring of the "Human Species" fan fame?

HARRY: Yes. Who are you?

KYLE: My name is Kyle, sir. My father sold fans, too. Maybe

you've heard of him. Gordon Williker?

HARRY: Gordy. Of course. We once discussed religion at Donald Farland's home.

COP: *PIPE DOWN AND SOUND OFF!!* (He rams his gun into Harry's stomach.)

HARRY: Ohhhhhhhhh!

PRISONERS: *ONE. TWO. THREE. FOUR. ONE. TWO. THREE. FOUR. ONE. TWO. THREE. FOUR. ONE...*

BLACKOUT.

(*Pause*, then lights up opposite stage, where JOSEPH appears, speaking with a police officer.)

OFFICER: So you're Joseph Goldring. I must admit I'm rather surprised to see you.

JOSEPH: How's my brother?

OFFICER: Not too well, I'm afraid. I thought the news about his family's success would raise his spirits. Quite the contrary. His stamina has never been lower.

(*Pause.*)

JOSEPH: I'm reconsidering your offer.

OFFICER: Oh?

JOSEPH: My brother doesn't deserve to die in that shithole.

OFFICER: You're not as stubborn as I thought. Good. It inspires me to see an artist give in. Shall you prefer our one year plan or nine over two?

JOSEPH: It doesn't matter.

OFFICER: Nine over two then. It's better.
(He removes a contract.)
I respect you. I want you to know that. Not everyone has talent. That's why artists are rarely executed here. Pity, there aren't more as soft as you.
(He hands JOSEPH the contract.)
Sign on the dotted line. Nine propaganda projects over two years in exchange for your brother's freedom.
(JOSEPH signs.)
Here are your crayons, "how to" book, and an apple. Congratulations.
(*Pause.*)
Welcome to our world, Mister Goldring.

NARRATOR: My father re-entered freedom on June 11. He stayed with Joseph only two miles from our home, but never came to visit. The word was he had contracted a rare disease while in prison which prevented him from sleeping. He soon began to dream while awake.

HARRY (dreaming): To hell with you and your world. A lifetime of creativity *can* be replaced by a second-rate school. Joseph. There are spiders on my throat. Kill them. Kill them! STAY AWAY FROM ME! Did you see him? YOU AND YOUR ROACH BODY KISSER!! Kill them, Joseph! You dirty stinking fish! You putrid fucking stump! KILL THEM!! **KILL THEM!!!**

NARRATOR: On August 3, Joseph refused to complete his first propaganda project for the government, as he and my father fled the law. After nine months of life on the run, father decided to stop at a small motel near Ocean Avenue. It was here, at one P.M., he and his brother decided to end it all.

(HARRY and JOSEPH sit at a table. A box of rat poison and two glasses are set before them. HARRY pours some poison into his glass and stirs. He then does the same for Joseph's glass.)

(*Pause.*)

HARRY: Farewell, Joseph. You've been a good and faithful brother. I love you.

(*Pause.* Then they slowly lift their glasses.)

HARRY: May we be wrong and there be a better place than this somewhere.

(They drink, then sit motionless for several seconds.)

(*Silence.*)

LIGHTS SLOWLY FADE TO BLACK.

(In the darkness, melancholy accordion music is heard. Lights rise to reveal two graves. JOSAPHENE, LITTLE HARRY and his four sisters, as well as MRS. MELISH, attend a funeral.)

JOSAPHENE: Your father always insisted on doing things his way, or not at all. He was as stubborn as a mule. (*Pause.*) Little Harry. You have great potential. Promise me you won't throw it away the way your dad did.

LITTLE HARRY: I promise.

(LITTLE HARRY removes the "Human Species" fan, which resembles a giant asshole, and places it on his father's grave site. He then places the non-conformist doll by the fan.)

BABY DOLL: *Fuck the bourgeoisie! Fuck the bourgeoisie!*

LITTLE HARRY (after a pause): So long, dad.

(*Silence,* as the Goldring family share a moment of reflection. After several seconds, the ACCORDION PLAYER steps forward and begins singing.)

ACCORDION PLAYER:
    And so the end has come for Harold Goldring
    whose life you've seen performed here on the stage.
    The fight he led to sabotage our habits
    no doubt will slowly fade away with age.

    His fans had been the form of his expression
    and they poked the heart of Christianity
    in a dream to break the shackles of oppression
    and stomp the chest of mediocrity.

    The truth he sought, in the end he's found -
    There's nothing more truthful than a corpse in the ground.

JOSAPHENE (sings):
    He racked his brain with thoughts about society
    but neglected both his children and his wife.
    Such pondering will only cause anxiety
    and fill one's days with headaches and with strife.

Man is man, he'll never change, and that is that!
Just forget about this revolution stuff.
Take what you can, grab the cash, and get real fat.
All the rest is nothing but a load of guff!

The truth he sought, in the end he's found -
There's nothing more truthful than a corpse in the ground.

THE ENTIRE CAST:
The truth he sought, in the end he's found -
There's nothing more truthful than a corpse in the ground.

BLACKOUT.

Nachthunde

Musiktheater
(2003)

Characters

Singing & Speaking Roles

Michael
Gustavo
An Arab Man
The Narrator
A Revolutionary Leader
Schmidt
Stanislaw
Little Michael

Silent Roles

Salvador Dalí
Two Old Men
An Elderly Woman
A Man in Rags
Wunderlich
Katarina

As well as...

Arabian men & women, soldiers, children, and a cocker spaniel.

1

A hot summer day.

Silence.

Like a dream, the following sounds fade in and out, sometimes overlapping each other: An announcement from a train station, distant and muffled; crashing ocean waves; voices of children laughing and playing; and dogs barking.

After a moment, a humming sound is heard. It grows in volume and intensity, continuing long after the other sounds have faded. It eventually becomes so loud and piercing, it is painful to the ear.

Suddenly...

Silence.

2

An estate in the desert.

Through an intense red light, the silhouettes of two young men appear, digging with shovels. The sound of their shovels plowing into the dirt echoes through the landscape.

As the digging continues, a brown glow is seen through the dust, illuminating an old-fashioned radio. The following broadcast is heard:

RADIO BROADCAST: *The two men recruited for the project are Michael Bashkiewicz, age 31, and Gustavo Octavio, age 27, both from the Los Angeles area. Digging started early yesterday morning at the Willenberg estate. So far there have been no signs of the late Jacob Willenberg's remains uncovered. However, several other objects were found including a number of bones believed to be of canine origin; and a book, badly decayed, the contents of which...*

The radio signal is lost. After a moment, one of the young men sets down his shovel and makes his way to a storage room. The sound of a large wooden door opening is heard…

3

Inside the storage room. The sun's rays flood through the open door, while the rest of the room remains in shadows.

The young man, MICHAEL BASHKIEWICZ, is taking a breather. He removes his cap and wipes some sweat from his forehead. He then takes a drink of water from his canteen.

Silence.

In the shadows, a small cocker spaniel appears. MICHAEL watches the dog for several seconds. At first he appears deeply moved, and then frightened.

MICHAEL (calling to the dog): Poochie.

After a moment, the dog vanishes. Enter GUSTAVO OCTAVIO, Michael's digging partner. He looks at MICHAEL, who seems startled.

GUSTAVO: What's the matter?

Pause.

MICHAEL: My dog…from when I was a kid…I just saw her here.

GUSTAVO (chuckles): What are you talking about?

(MICHAEL looks toward a table where some of the objects he and GUSTAVO had dug up were placed. He notices that something is missing.)

MICHAEL: The bones…

(GUSTAVO takes a closer look. At first he focuses his attention on an area of the table where some bones were placed, now missing. Then he notices a rather large art book, which appears to be brand new.)

GUSTAVO: What's this? (*Pause.*) Where did this come from?

Silence.

(Both men are confused. It appears as if a living dog and a brand new book have somehow replaced the canine bones and decayed book that were dug up earlier.)

MICHAEL: There's something crazy going on here. It must be coming from the earth where we're digging… (*Pause.*) I'm getting out of here, before it drives me completely mad!

Frantic, MICHAEL flees the room. A heavy breeze is heard. Soon, another sound is introduced: A train raging through the night…

4

A train compartment, late in the evening.

MICHAEL is seen sitting with a number of Arabian men and women, several of whom are wearing turbans and other exotic headdresses. One of the men begins talking with MICHAEL.

ARAB MAN: Have you heard? Salvador Dalí is on this train tonight.

MICHAEL: What?

ARAB MAN: Salvador Dalí. He's here. On this train.

Pause.

MICHAEL: But Dalí's dead. He died in 1989.

ARAB MAN: No. I'm afraid you're mistaken. Dalí is still alive, although he's very old now. You see, he's traveling tonight to the Willenberg estate, where he's going to bury himself. They say there's something magical in the earth there.

After a pause, the train compartment door opens and Salvador Dalí enters, surrounded by an entourage of Arabs. He is old and corpse-like, being pushed in a wheelchair. There are oxygen tubes connected to his nostrils, and his body is shaking uncontrollably. MICHAEL looks on in horror. The smell of death overwhelms the compartment.

BLACKOUT.

The train continues raging through the night...

5

Soft piano is heard. After a moment, enter GUSTAVO, who sings the following lieder:

> In the night I saw her face
> Though it was distant and unrecognizable.
> She smiled and I felt her breath
> Before she faded into the shadows.
> I, too, was in the shadows
> Surrounded by friends and pets from my youth.
> Soon, they also faded from my memory
> Leaving me helpless and alone in the night.

6

Quiet for several seconds.

Suddenly, a collage of automobile horns is heard, bursting from every direction. In addition, red lights flash on and off. A NARRATOR appears and begins telling the following story. He is accompanied by two interpreters, who translate into German and French.

NARRATOR: On a warm summer evening, our main character, Michael Bashkiewicz, age 31, was crossing a street in the city of Los Angeles. The noise and traffic of the city disrupted his thoughts, although he tried his best to shut them out. Suddenly, from the pavement below, the memories of past pedestrians began lighting up like tiny fireflies. One memory was of a small boy in 1969 going to the movies with his mother, and then eating lunch at Clifton's Cafeteria. Another recalled a girl in 1927 being molested by her older brother. As the memories glittered like a cluster of stars in the sky, a rather large light jumped from the pavement into Michael's hand, and began quivering like a snowflake. It was the memory of an old man who had walked on that exact spot of the street in 1979. It began recounting for Michael an incident the man experienced many years before...

The memory is presented:

June 28, 1947. An unknown country.
A group of revolutionaries are preparing for battle. The sounds of gunfire and distant explosions are heard.

REVOLUTIONARY LEADER: The time is now upon us, comrades. Soon the *victims* in our society will become the *victors*. Is everyone ready?

(All answer "yes" except for one man, who answers "no".)

Pause.

LEADER: Who said "no"?

VOICE: I did.

(A soldier named SCHMIDT steps forward.)

Pause.

LEADER: What's going on, Schmidt?

SCHMIDT: I've lost hope in the revolution. I'm not going to fight anymore. It hurts me to admit it, but I have to be honest. I just don't feel your passion anymore. I don't believe things will ever change.

Silence.

LEADER: I feel sorry for you, Schmidt. (*Pause.*) The world *can* be changed, and is *in need* of change. (*Pause.*) Come on, comrades. Forget about him. Our time for action has come! (He lifts a rifle and shouts one final battle cry.) SOLDIERS OF THE OPPRESSED, TAKE CONTROL OF YOUR DESTINY!

(The revolutionaries charge into battle. The gunfire and explosions grow louder. In addition, the following sounds fade in and out, overlapping each other: Planes flying overhead; roaring thunder; sirens; screams; and speeches by historical figures such as Adolph Hitler and Josef Stalin.)

(As the above sounds fade, SCHMIDT is seen by himself, lost in thought. After a moment, he removes a small can opener and opens a can of dog food. A golden retriever appears. SCHMIDT spoons the food into a bowl and watches as the dog begins eating. He pets the animal tenderly.)

Silence.

The red sun is setting.

NARRATOR: Moved by the memory, Michael took it home and placed it in a jar, where he kept it for several months.

LIGHTS SLOWLY FADE.

7

The desert estate. Dusk.

Shovels and other digging equipment have been left abandoned.

Quiet.

Only a gentle breeze and periodic whispers can be heard.

In the dirt, a white dove is seen. Injured and unable to fly, it desperately flaps its wings, jerking and shaking.

Pause.

In the distance, the faint sounds of children playing are heard.

A little boy enters, eating a blueberry tart. He explores the area, picking up a bone and an old clay pot. After a moment, he wanders into the storage room. A large wooden door slams shut behind him...

8

Inside the storage room, which now appears much bigger. The lighting melts into an intense red, dark and with shadows. Unbearable heat.

In addition, several new sounds are introduced, including: Distorted moans; inaudible voices in different languages; dogs howling; and periodic crashes.

Like a nightmare, a parade of strange characters moves among the shadows. Multiple episodes unfold simultaneously. The little boy observes, and sometimes participates in, the activities which follow.

The first of these episodes reveals an old man crawling in slow motion. Every move he makes is deliberate to the point of being painful. He eventually turns onto his back, like an upside down turtle, and moves his hands desperately upward.

Second episode: Several children appear, playing with string puppets that resemble little dogs.

Third episode: An elderly woman enters, struggling to push a dusty wheel barrow that contains the following: Old toys; newspapers and magazines from the 1960s; broken up lawn sprinklers; and a soldier's helmet from World War II. A few of the children make their way to the wheel barrow, getting a closer look at some of the toys.

Fourth episode: A second man is seen crawling in slow motion. Like the first one, he ends up on his back, moving his hands desperately upward.

Fifth episode: A man in rags appears, pulling a large wooden wagon. The wagon is filled with canine bones, old art books, blueberry tarts, and various human limbs.

Sixth episode: Four men, barely visible in the shadows, sing the following songs:

> 1st Song
> *Poochie Puppy Poochie Puppy*
> *KITTY WITTIE*
> *Poochie Puppy Poochie Puppy*
> *KITTY WITTIE*
> *HOLLYSHITAROLLY!*
>
> 2nd Song
> *HOLLYSHITAROLLY!*
> *POOCHIE PUPPY!*
> *POOCHIE PUPPY KITTY WITTIE!*
> *POOCHIE PUPPY!*

As the episodes progress, the humming sound from Scene 1 is heard. It builds slowly in volume and intensity, eventually becoming so loud and piercing, it is painful to the ear.

Rays of light cut through the red shadows, accompanied by a haunting fog. The heat has become even more extreme.

In the end, each of the episodes moves toward a conclusion, with the characters eventually disappearing. Only the two men on their backs remain, desperately reaching upward in slow motion.

The humming sound continues for more than a minute. Then, suddenly…

Silence.

BLACKOUT.

9

The NARRATOR appears, accompanied by his interpreters.

NARRATOR: On a quiet evening in August, by a pond in the woods, Michael decided to set free the memory he had found a few months before.

MICHAEL is seen, holding a jar. He opens it, releasing the memory. A light, like a firefly, hovers in front of him, before floating into the distance.

Silence.

As MICHAEL stands alone, he becomes absorbed by the sounds and smells of the woods. Meanwhile, in the shadows, two children appear, running through the night. Their giggles can be heard.

The children (a boy and a girl) eventually sit down on the ground. They begin touching each other's bodies for the first time, displaying a great deal of curiosity and innocence. MICHAEL watches quietly from afar.

Silence, except for the children's giggles.

From another part of the woods, MICHAEL suddenly becomes distracted by what sounds like a person crying. He makes his way down a path to investigate, and discovers a FREAK sitting on a stone. The Freak's face and body are badly deformed.

MICHAEL: Hello. (*Pause.*) Why are you crying?

(The FREAK does not respond. MICHAEL hands him a small

handkerchief, to wipe his tears. Timid and unsure of Michael's sincerity, the FREAK hesitates, before taking it.)

FREAK: Thank you.

Pause.

MICHAEL: My name's Michael.

FREAK (after loudly blowing his nose): I'm Stanislaw.

MICHAEL: Is there anything I can do to help?

STANISLAW (collecting himself): Well...it would be nice to have someone to talk with. Would you mind?

MICHAEL: No.

STANISLAW: I have a story I'd like to tell, about something that happened to me. It might do me good to get it off my chest. (STANISLAW takes a moment to compose his thoughts.) Let me tell you my story.
(His mind begins drifting into the past.)
Several months ago, I met a woman named Katarina in these woods. She was hiking with her dog, and I was sitting here, on this stone. The moment I saw her, something happened to me. A strange excitement rushed through my body, and my heart began pounding. She was so beautiful. (*Pause.*) I decided to remain quiet and pretend not to see her. You see, most people find me hideous and are frightened by me, and I figured she would react in the same way. So I remained silent. (*Short pause.*) She came over to me. I was so nervous I didn't know what to say. When I turned my head to face her, I heard a gasp, but she didn't scream or run

away. Surprisingly, she continued talking with me. (*Pause.*) She was so beautiful. Her face was so soft and gentle, and her eyes were like the eyes of a deer. When I saw her up close, she was like a child, so innocent, and yet so sensual and womanly. I could hardly contain my excitement. (*Brief pause.*) Strange as it seemed, she enjoyed talking with me, about art and philosophy and life, and about our love of animals and nature. It turned out we had many things in common, and before I knew it, several hours had passed. We just kept walking through the woods, and talking so openly and honestly. I had never felt so comfortable with another person before. (*Pause.*) I wanted to see her again, but wasn't sure how I should go about it. If I asked her for a date, I thought I might scare her off. So I approached it as a friend, and suggested maybe getting together one afternoon for a walk with her dog. (*Pause.*) She overwhelmed me. Everything about her made me feel joyous inside - Her eyes and her lips, her hair, the tone of her voice, the way her chest moved when she breathed, her smile. I was falling completely and uncontrollably in love with her. (*Brief pause.*) My eyes focused on her lips. They were so soft and red and luscious. I knew I was taking a chance, but I couldn't help myself. I *had* to touch and taste her skin. I quickly pressed my lips against hers. My body started to quiver. The taste from her lips was sublime. (*Brief pause.*) Unfortunately, my ecstasy was brief. She pulled away from me and suddenly became quiet. I could tell that I had frightened her. (*Brief pause.*) From that moment on, everything changed. I tried talking with her, but she remained quiet and withdrawn. I could see in her eyes that, as a friend, she had been willing to accept me, but the thought of any romance with me repulsed her. (*Pause.*) During the following weeks, I tried to contact her many times, but she wanted nothing to do with me. (*Brief pause.*) It's been more than four months now, and I still can't stop thinking about her. It tortures me to know that I'll never be able to love her. (He breaks down, crying. *Long pause.*) Earlier today, while in a market, I noticed a Playboy magazine with a woman on the cover who resembles Katarina. I bought it and brought it here. I've been studying the photos, imagining that the naked body is her, and that I'm finally able to see the flesh of the woman I love.

(MICHAEL consoles STANISLAW.)

Silence.

(The night hours have dwindled away. It is now daybreak. Suddenly, hundreds of tiny explosions illuminate the horizon.)

STANISLAW (pointing toward the sky): What is it?

MICHAEL: It's the millions of dreams that are dying the moment their creators awake this morning.

(MICHAEL and STANISLAW, as well as the two children, watch the sky, deeply moved by what they see.)

LIGHTS SLOWLY FADE.

10

Soft piano is heard. After a moment, enter GUSTAVO, who sings the following lieder:

> *Through the mist I heard a sigh*
> *Warning me of an intruder's presence.*
> *Covered in dust, his eyes were shut*
> *Dreaming of spiders and toys in the dirt.*
> *Nervously, I crawled past him*
> *Entering a cloud of exotic perfume.*
> *There, a shadow caressed my cheek gently*
> *And whispered softly into my ear.*
> *"Do you remember me?"*
> *"Do you remember when you first touched me?"*
> *"Do you remember when I touched you?"*
> *My mind could no longer recall the past*
> *And the shadow vanished into the haze from the moon.*

11

The NARRATOR appears, accompanied by his interpreters.

NARRATOR: That morning, triggered by the sight of the exploding dreams, Michael's memory drifted back in time, recalling an incident he experienced when he was 7 years old. It was during the summer of 1972, while he and his family were vacationing in the mountains of California...

(MICHAEL appears, telling his story to STANISLAW.)

MICHAEL: I remember sitting by the edge of a lake with my brother and a few other kids. It was dusk. Suddenly, I looked up, and in the distance, just above the lake, these strange figures appeared, dancing in the air. Their bodies were transparent, like ghosts, but with bright, vibrant colors, and their reflections flickered on the water below. It was almost like a movie, but there was no movie screen.

(A group of children, including Michael as a 7 year old, is seen.)

LITTLE MICHAEL (pointing to the transparent figures): Look!

(At first the children appear somewhat frightened, but are quickly overcome by a sense of curiosity and pleasure.)

MICHAEL: To our delight, the figures began acting out a collection of stories. Some were adventure tales set during the war, and others were wacky comedies loaded with slapstick.

(Like characters in a silent movie projected against the sky, the ghost figures entertain the children with a comedy routine. A transparent OLD LADY appears.)

FIRST SKIT PERFORMED BY GHOSTS IN THE SKY

An OLD LADY with a cane is walking down a path, when she spots a scrumptious-looking blueberry tart on the ground. Rigid and aching, she laboriously bends to pick it up, but just as she's about to grab it, the tart suddenly moves, and the OLD LADY falls over.

Determined, the OLD LADY struggles to get up, and once again pursues the tart. But, like before, just as she's about to snatch it, the tart moves, and the OLD LADY falls.

In an attempt to outsmart the tart, the OLD LADY pretends to have lost interest. She puckers her wrinkled lips as if whistling, and looks the other way. Periodically, she turns slowly, trying to sneak up on the tart, but each time the elusive treat also moves.

Suddenly, the OLD LADY leaps toward the tart, which escapes in the nick of time by flying upward. Frustrated and worn out, she pounds her fists into the ground and cries, before looking up into the sky, as if to ask God, "Why are you torturing me?" Just then, the blueberry tart falls from above and splatters in the Old Lady's face.

(The children erupt with laughter.)

LITTLE GIRL: Did you see that?!

CHUBBY BOY: Mmm, that tart looked good.

MICHAEL: One of our favorite stories that evening began with the words "Brown Balls" written across the sky. It featured a German soldier named Wunderlich, who had set out to capture a little boy guilty of stealing his grapes.

SECOND SKIT PERFORMED BY GHOSTS IN THE SKY
"BROWN BALLS"

WUNDERLICH prepares a trap, with grapes for bait. He is fat, and wears a military uniform draped with medals. A helmet with a spike sticking out of its top sits on his head.

A LITTLE BOY appears, and begins devouring the grapes. As he pulls a juicy grape from its stem, a large basket falls from above, trapping the LITTLE BOY.

WUNDERLICH, excited about his catch, lifts the basket and grabs the boy by his hair. Frightened, the child points to something in the distance, and when WUNDERLICH turns to look, the LITTLE BOY kicks him in the rear end.

Infuriated, WUNDERLICH tries to grab the boy again, but, instead, accidentally knocks the grapes to the ground. When he bends over to pick them up, the LITTLE BOY farts in Wunderlich's face - a gas so powerful, it sends the soldier flying through the air.

(Again, the children roar with laughter.)

CHUBBY BOY: Take that!

(LITTLE MICHAEL and a few of the other boys engage in horseplay. After a moment, WUNDERLICH reappears in the sky. He smiles as he removes a revolver, which he points toward the children. The barrel of the weapon stretches, like Pinocchio's nose, across the lake, stopping right against Little Michael's forehead. Overwhelmed by fear, the child freezes.)

Silence.

(But WUNDERLICH is only playing, taking great pleasure in

watching a bead of sweat dribble down the left cheek on Little Michael's face.)

BLACKOUT.

12

An eruption of laughter is heard.

AH HA HA HA! AH HA HA HA! AH HA HA HA!

Ho ho ho. He he he. Ho ho ho. He he he.

AH HA HA HA! AH HA HA HA! AH HA HA HA!

Several clown-like faces, distorted and grotesque, appear in the shadows. In addition, a chorus of dogs barking and howling is heard, followed by the sounds of a child crying.

Eventually, the faces disappear, and this brief interlude of laughs, barks and cries begins to fade, while a new sound is introduced: An Arabic singer performing a haunting chant...

13

The desert estate. Dusk.

A group of Arab men and women, several of whom are wearing turbans and other exotic headdresses, have gathered. The haunting chant continues.

Salvador Dalí is seen, lying in the dirt. Like a wounded animal taking his final breaths, he struggles desperately to bury himself. His movements are painfully slow, as he grabs piles of earth, and pours them over his body. The Arab men and women watch closely.

Silence, except for the chanting.

MICHAEL appears, observing the burial. On the ground, by his feet, are piles of canine bones, as well as a few blueberry tarts. After a moment, he picks up one of the bones and examines it, before placing it in his pocket, and making his way to the storage room.

A large wooden door opening is heard...

14

Inside the storage room. The Arabic chanting has faded into the distance. Soon, it is quiet.

Pause.

MICHAEL wanders through the shadows, which appear endless. As he makes his way deeper into the space, splashing water is heard, accompanied by dancing blue lights. To Michael's surprise, he discovers a swimming pool, lit only by a lamp under the water.

KATARINA, a beautiful German girl in her 20's, emerges from the pool, wearing an old-fashioned bathing suit, the type worn by women during the 1920's. MICHAEL watches with nervous anticipation, as she slowly pushes her wet hair back, revealing her soft, angelic face.

Silence.

Entranced by Katarina's beauty, MICHAEL becomes speechless. Suddenly, a small ball rolls before him. It is a ball he and his childhood friends used to play with many years before. After a moment of recollection, he tosses the ball by the pool. Like a ballerina, KATARINA dances gracefully, before diving and catching it. She then rolls it back to MICHAEL.

The two begin playing like children, often giggling and making funny faces at one another. MICHAEL throws a succession of passes by the pool, each of which KATARINA dances toward and catches with remarkable grace and prowess, sometimes even doing back flips and cartwheels.

Filled with joy and a child-like enthusiasm, MICHAEL heaves a long pass. KATARINA dances, and makes a tremendous leap, but trips and smashes into the ground. She lies motionless for several seconds, before struggling to get up. Like a newborn pony attempting to stand for the first time, her legs quiver, as she strains to lift herself. She collapses, and then tries again, finally succeeding.

MICHAEL rushes to Katarina's side, deeply concerned. He feels somewhat responsible for what has happened, and can't stop apologizing. But KATARINA presses her index finger against Michael's lips, making the sound, "shhhhhhhhhhh." She then caresses his cheek gently.

By the edge of the pool, a small cocker spaniel appears. It is Michael's dog from when he was a child. KATARINA pets the dog, and then puts a leash on it. She looks at MICHAEL one final time, before turning and walking away with the dog, disappearing into the shadows.

MICHAEL stands alone, his image withering in the darkness.

Silence.

LIGHTS SLOWLY FADE

Mondvögel

Musiktheater
(2005)

Characters

Michael
A Young Woman
Various Ghost Figures

1

The ocean, late at night. The sky is dark, lit only by a full moon. The gentle rippling of water can be heard.

MICHAEL, a man in his forties, appears. In deep blue light, which dances with the rhythm of the sea, he walks slowly, up to his ankles in water. His movements are deliberate, almost in slow-motion. While he appears lost in thought, his senses are well aware of his surroundings. He stops periodically to observe the sky, and to feel the coolness of the water covering his feet.

Long Silence.

Behind the moon, a red haze appears, and begins bleeding downward. MICHAEL watches with a combination of curiosity and concern.

Suddenly, the moon breaks apart into several small pieces, which are instantly transformed into white birds. The creatures fly about madly, flapping their wings in an uncontrolled frenzy. After a moment, they disappear, leaving MICHAEL alone in the dark, illuminated only by a faint streak of red that remains in the sky.

2

Several ghost figures appear in the shadows. Some have miner's helmets with red lights beaming from them, while others have lanterns, also red, hanging from their necks, or strapped over their shoulders. With bodies covered in black, the phantoms crawl on the ground, like an army of insects. Whispers are heard, as well as periodic moans. As the ghosts continue their night crawl, additional sounds are heard, including distant crashes and stomping feet.

After a moment, a beam of light illuminates the following...

3

A YOUNG WOMAN is seen, sleeping on the ground. She is nude, with drapes of white muslin hanging behind her. On her face is a look of calm, as she dreams peacefully.

Silence.

The shadow of an arm and hand appears, stretching across the ground, and eventually reaching the young woman's body. It fondles her breasts and private part, at times with tenderness, but at other moments with a sense of sinister violation.

Distant moans are heard, though it is difficult to tell whether they express pain or pleasure.

As the shadow hand continues its exploration of the woman's body, several other hands appear, reaching up from the ground. Their fingers wiggle slowly, as if they are grasping to touch something beautiful and essential.

Suddenly, blood emerges from the drapes of muslin and begins dripping downward.

Silence.

BLACKOUT.

4

Lights up to reveal a procession of ghost figures, all wearing masks. Some of their faces are clown-like, while others are deformed and grotesque. The phantoms stagger and fall into one another, displaying a great deal of weariness, like victims in a prison camp. A few begin climbing upward on rope ladders, as another dangles his body over a wooden swing, swaying back and forth.

The sound of soldiers marching is heard, as well as inaudible voices, some of which are screaming. A great deal of confusion and commotion ensues.

MICHAEL appears, no longer wearing a shirt. His body is awkward and contorted, like a figure in an Egon Schiele painting. His movements are in slow motion.

Three of the phantoms surround MICHAEL and begin dowsing him with cups of blood. As the blood splatters onto Michael's chest, he jerks backward, as if his flesh has just been pierced, or as if a nerve in his brain has been splintered, causing his body to spasm. With each dowsing, he grimaces with pain, stumbling and fighting to keep his balance. Again, all of his movements are in slow motion.

Overwhelmed by the assault, MICHAEL begins falling to the ground, letting out a horrific cry on the way down. When his body finally hits the earth, a massive eruption is heard and felt, like a devastating earthquake. The aftershocks continue for several seconds, before eventually fading.

SUDDEN DARKNESS.

Silence.

5

An old Super 8 film is projected against a backdrop. It portrays a family during the 1960s, with several children laughing and playing.

The YOUNG WOMAN appears, walking among the projected images. She is now clothed, and displays an almost childlike innocence.

In the shadows, MICHAEL rises slowly. He looks toward the YOUNG WOMAN, clearly effected by her presence. As he struggles to move toward her, the film comes to an end. Flickering lights are seen for several seconds.

Silence.

6

MICHAEL and the YOUNG WOMAN remain in the same positions. Lights fade slowly into a deep red.

On each side of the YOUNG WOMAN, a ghost figure appears and sets up a miniature spiral slide (about 3 feet tall). Into these gadgets, red marbles are poured, which roll and twist downward with a thunderous roar.

As MICHAEL watches, his body suddenly becomes paralyzed. A look of desperation overwhelms his face, as he sees the YOUNG WOMAN walking away slowly. Above him, a white light begins swinging back and forth, like a pendulum.

After a moment, the setting returns to the ocean, late at night.

Once again, the gentle rippling of water can be heard, while the lighting dances with the rhythm of the sea. However, this time an intense red remains, accentuated by violent heat and steam.

MICHAEL continues watching the YOUNG WOMAN, who walks slowly into the distance, eventually disappearing. He remains completely still, as if his heart has stopped beating. Above him, the white light continues swinging back and forth.

Long Silence.

Suddenly, several white birds reappear, flying chaotically in the sky.

LIGHTS SLOWLY FADE.

The Final Thoughts of Stanislaw Bashkiewicz

A Short Play
(1991)

Characters

Stanislaw
An Old Man
The Ringmaster
3 Dancing Assholes
5 Audience Members

This play was written on June 28, 1991, the same day its author died.

Scene One

The Beard

Shadows.

A young Man named STANISLAW sits in a chair. His eyes are closed. To his left, a television monitor projects images from the space as they occur. Behind him, a large piece of muslin hangs.

Three musicians create eerie, electronic noises. They begin softly, then build, *build,* ***build!***

Chaos swallows the space.

Suddenly...STANISLAW stands and, holding his head firmly in his hands, lets out a horrifying cry –

STANISLAW: **AHHHHHHHHHHHHHHHHHHHHHH HHHHHHHHHHHHHHHHHHHHHHHHHHHH...**

An OLD MAN bursts into the room and screams directly in Stanislaw's face.

OLD MAN: **SHUT THE FUCK UP! ARE YOU OUTA YOUR FUCKING MIND?! WHAT THE FUCK'S A MATTER WITH YOU?! LOOK AT THIS FUCKING PLACE! ARE YOU FUCKING CRAZY?! DO YOU FUCKING UNDERSTAND?! LISTEN TO ME! I SAID LISTEN TO ME! YOU STUPID FUCKING RETARD! YOU DUMB FUCKING MORON! DO YOU FUCKING COMPREHEND?! I SAID LISTEN TO ME! YOU STUPID PIECE OF SHIT! YOU DUMB FUCKING IDIOT! YOUR BRAINS ARE FUCKING**

COLD! YOUR HEAD IS FUCKING DEAD! DON'T YOU FUCKING SEE?! DON'T YOU FUCKING SEE?! DON'T YOU FUCKING SEE?!

When the OLD MAN reaches the sentence "Look at this fucking place!" – in particular, the words "at this" – an AUDIENCE MEMBER stands and begins screaming, too. She makes her way down to STANISLAW and, like the OLD MAN, screams directly in his face.

AUDIENCE MEMBER: **ARE YOU A FUCKING MARXIST?! THEN WHY THE FUCK DO YOU READ BRECHT?! ARE YOU A FUCKING REPUBLICAN?! I DOUBT YOU KNOW WHO THE FUCK YOU ARE! DO YOU SUPPORT SKINNER? YOU SAID YOU WERE A FUCKING BEHAVIORIST! DID YOU READ NIETZSCHE?! THEN MAYBE YOU SHOULD GO BACK TO SCHOOL! ARE YOU A FUCKING SURREALIST?! I'D FUCKING SAY NO! DO YOU ACT FUCKING ROMANTIC? THAT'S A POSSIBILITY! ARE YOU TRYING TO BE A PARADOX?! THAT'S FUCKING ABSURD! I DON'T THINK YOU KNOW WHO THE FUCK YOU ARE! I DON'T THINK YOU KNOW WHO THE FUCK YOU ARE!**

When the AUDIENCE MEMBER reaches the sentence "I doubt you know who the fuck you are!" – in particular, the words "doubt you" – a SECOND AUDIENCE MEMBER, an attractive young woman with freckles on her cheeks, stands and begins shouting. She, too, makes her way down to the stage and yells directly in Stanislaw's face.

SECOND AUDIENCE MEMBER: **DON'T YOU FUCKING SPEAK TO ME! YOU STUPID FUCKING JOKE! I'LL FUCK WHOEVER I FUCKING WANT TO! I'LL CALL WHEN I FUCKING NEED YOU! RIGHT NOW GET THE FUCK**

OUT OF MY LIFE! YOU IDIOTIC SHIT! YOU GULLIBLE LITTLE FUCK! I NEVER FUCKING SAID YOU COULD FUCK ME! I DON'T EVEN FUCKING KNOW YOU! YOU ANNOYING PIECE OF DUMP! YOU INSIGNIFICANT FUCKING SCREW! RIGHT NOW GET THE FUCK OUT OF MY LIFE!

Suddenly...an incredible squeal is heard. It bombards the space with a storm of violence. It gradually decreases in speed, getting slower...and slower...and slower, like a phonograph drained of its power. Everyone begins moving in slow motion. Their voices diminish into deep, spiritless moans. In addition, distant whispers and distorted sounds are heard. The entire space is stripped of its energy. Soon, all is frozen.

Silence.

After a moment, a voice from a loud speaker is heard. It says the following:

"All that is forgotten, it must be real. And all that is real...must have a beard."

Silence.

BLACKOUT.

As the blackout occurs, the television monitor turns to static. It continues for several seconds, then...

Silence.

DARKNESS.

Scene Two

The Number

A RINGMASTER enters, wearing a dark tuxedo, top hat, and handlebar mustache.

RINGMASTER: Good evening, you little putz, you little worm! I'm going to show a show the whole entire world is dying to see! Are you a happy camper? Do you feel glee eight days of the week? Are you cheery inside your hair, lungs and ass? Well all that can be taken care of! In one short minute you can be a miserable dump just like everyone else! WHAT DO YOU SAY TO THAT?!

MUSIC!

RINGMASTER: Well this is what we say...

The RINGMASTER performs a number in the flavor of an old Busby Berkeley routine. He is accompanied by 3 DANCING ASSHOLES. The three musicians join in with kazoos and duck calls.

>We're so happy that you're sad
>*la la la la la la la*
>We're so happy that you're sad
>*la la la la la la la*
>It makes us feel so bloody glad
>*la la la la la la la*
>We're so happy that you're sad

You make us sick to be alive
la la la la la la la
Like chafed legs on Saturday night
la la la la la la la
We're so happy that you're sad
la la la la la la la
We're so happy that...
You're...
Saaaaaaaaaaaaaaaaaaaaaaaaaaaaaaaaaadddddd
la la la la la la la la la la la la la la la la la la la la la la la la la
Wooooooooooo!

Scene Three

The Alleviation

RINGMASTER: Come, my son. Take my hand and relieve yourself of this giant pot of shit. I am here to lead you. I am your guide.

ASSHOLE #1 (to Stanislaw): Here. Swallow these pills.

ASSHOLE #2: No. Down this egg.

ASSHOLE #1: Pills come before egg.

ASSHOLE #2: I'm afraid you're mistaken.

RINGMASTER: Please. Don't squabble. You're *all* my friends. First: *Egg* must always be eaten to ensure soothing of the stomach's inner surface. (He shoves an egg into Stanislaw's face.) Next: Pills are swallowed to enhance the rate of blood flow. (He pops some pills into Stanislaw's mouth.) How do you feel?

STANISLAW (after some hesitation): I...

ASSHOLE #1: Time's up! Now stand straight.

ASSHOLE #2: No. Crouch low.

ASSHOLE #3: Open your eyes.

ASSHOLE #2: They *are* open.

ASSHOLE #3: Well close them then.

ASSHOLE #1: Do *this!* (She rubs her belly while patting her head.)

ASSHOLE #2: Now tilt your head.

ASSHOLE #1: Relax.

ASSHOLE #3: Wiggle your nose.

ASSHOLE #1: Say *ahhhhhhhhhhh!*

RINGMASTER: Take my hand. (He displays a revolver in his palm.) Go on. Take it. (*Pause.*) You need to *trust* if we're going to succeed.

ASSHOLE #1: Go ahead. Don't be afraid.

ASSHOLE #2: Take it.

ASSHOLE #3: We're only trying to help you.

ASSHOLE #2: Take it.

VOICE FROM OFFSTAGE: Take it.

RINGMASTER: I am here to lead you.

ASSHOLE #3: Take it.

ASSHOLE #1: Take it.

ASSHOLE #2: Take it.

AUDIENCE MEMBER: ***TAKE IT!!!!!!!!!!!!!!!!!!!!!!!!!!!!***

Silence.

(STANISLAW grabs the revolver.)

RINGMASTER: Congratulations, son. You're going to be free.

A snare drum roll is heard for several seconds. Then the first sixteen bars or so from *Auld Lang Syne* are performed. The music is demented, like the players are drunk. In addition, duck calls, wacky horns, fart sounds, and laughs are heard. The RINGMASTER prepares STANISLAW for his final task. The 3 ASSHOLES assist in straightening Stanislaw's collar, combing his hair, and brushing his teeth. After appropriate provisions, they reassuringly escort STANISLAW to his chair.

RINGMASTER (sings):
*Should auld acquaintance be forgot
And never brought to mind?
Should auld acquaintance be forgot
And days of auld lang syne?*

All of the participants, as well as numerous audience members, join in singing. Everyone comforts STANISLAW as they guide the revolver into his mouth.

EVERYONE:
*And days of auld lang syne, my dear,
And days of auld lang syne
Should auld acquaintance be forgot
And days of auld lang syne*

The lights are slowly dimming. Soon there is only a spotlight on STANISLAW, creating his silhouette against the muslin.

Silence.

A loud gun blast is heard.

Stanislaw's body flings backward while red liquid splatters across the muslin.

A bucket of small, red marbles is knocked over. A loud thunder is heard as the marbles bounce and roll across the floor. Once the motion of the marbles has come to a complete stop...

ABSOLUTE STILLNESS.

on his face there was a look of relief
a relaxing after great fatigue
his eyes and mouth were open...but no one could see

Appendix: Collaborations

The Last of the Living Surrealists (with Gustavo Octavio)

The Hobo Screenplay (with Gustavo Octavio)

Seehunde (with Shigeru Kan-no)

Note from the author:

The Last of the Living Surrealists and *The Hobo Screenplay* were both written during the spring of 1989, a special period when, along with my close friend, Gustavo Octavio, I discovered Surrealism. These experiments were created under the spell of the 1920s Paris group, in particular the works of Luis Buñuel and Salvador Dalí, and owe a great deal to their inspiration. Sadly, just as our surrealist awakening was taking place, Dalí passed away, which, in part, prompted us to create these pieces. Trying our best to follow the principles of Surrealism, we conjured up images, dreams and desires from the depths of our collective subconscious, refusing to censor ourselves in any way, no matter how grotesque or blasphemous the results. We also disregarded a conventional storytelling approach, and refused to impose on our discoveries any logical meaning. Just like what Buñuel and Dalí had experienced during their collaboration on *Un Chien Andalou* sixty years before, Gustavo and I never had one disagreement. We created together with great excitement, as if we were of one mind and imagination, with one mission. Whatever the merits of these two works may be, they represent for me a youthful time of exploration, discovery, freedom and friendship. For this reason, I have chosen to include them in the present collection.

The Last of the Living Surrealists contains a brief snippet from André Breton's *First Surrealist Manifesto* (1924).

Seehunde was written for the composer Shigeru Kan-no, who supplied it with an impressive original score. Some of its images were later reinterpreted and included in the slightly longer Musiktheater *Nachthunde*.

The Last of the Living Surrealists

A Movement Piece by Todd Bash & Gustavo Octavio
(1989)

Yoni and Moni were born in West Covina, California, the United States of America, on June 28, 1907. They traveled to Paris during the 1920s, where they studied dance and became part of the Surrealist movement. They were close friends with Luis Buñuel, Salvador Dalí, Rene Magritte, Joan Miro, Man Ray and André Breton. They broke with the group in 1930, opposing its links to the Communist Party, which they found at odds with the true spirit of Surrealism. They have since settled in Los Angeles, California, where they remain dedicated to *changing life*, and to exploring the depths of the subconscious mind.

Other characters that appear in this play are *a doctor who wears white, three audience members,* and *a man in nun's clothing.*

SCENE ONE.

The sound of a heartbeat is heard in the shadows.

YONI and MONI appear, sitting back to back, like two babies in a womb. They have stockings over their heads, and an umbilical cord connecting their belly buttons. They slowly roll their heads.

A man, known as THE DOCTOR, who has tape over his mouth, sharpens a knife. An eerie light shines down on him.

The heartbeat continues. Then, *suddenly*, it stops.

Silence.

THE DOCTOR makes his way to YONI and MONI. He slices their umbilical cord with his knife, then removes their stockings and stamps each on the forehead with an ink stamp. YONI and MONI look on in fright, as THE DOCTOR gathers his things and exits.

Silence.

SUDDENLY, loud, fast polka music is heard.

YONI and MONI jump to their feet. They clap their hands three times, then, in unison, look left and right, and left and right again. YONI looks back left and is surprised to see MONI standing there. Both men do double takes and jump in fear.

The dancers begin hopping backwards, moving in opposite directions, shaking their fists up and down. Next, in an exaggerated walk, or perhaps jog, they crisscross, before spinning, with elbows out.

Finally, they hop out with their knees together, and their fingers in their noses. When they meet, MONI orders YONI to the ground, where he begins crawling back and forth like a dog, periodically lifting his leg to urinate, while MONI does a Russian dance, jumping and kicking, and ultimately hopping across the stage. At one point, YONI crawls through the hopping Moni's legs.

Suddenly...the music stops.

SCENE TWO.

(YONI and MONI speak directly to the audience.)

YONI: Hello. My name is Yoni.

MONI: Hello. My name is Moni.

YONI AND MONI (together): And we're surrealist dancers.

(They close their eyes, but continue speaking directly to the audience. YONI begins, and then, after a sentence, MONI starts to echo him.)

YONI: We developed our style in 1920s Paris, where we became part of the Surrealist Movement. *Imagination, folly, dream, surrender to the dark forces of the unconscious, and recourse to the marvelous is here opposed, and preferred. To all that arises from necessity. From a logical order. From the reasonable.* Luis Buñuel. Dead. July 29, 1983. He was 83 years old. Salvador Dalí. Dead. He suffered his final years from painful burns. André Breton. Dead. He crossed the line between art and politics, and, consequently, contradicted his own teachings. Max Ernst. Dead. Joan Miro. Dead. Paul Eluard. Dead. Rene Magritte. Dead. (*Pause.*) *Living and ceasing to live are imaginary solutions. Existence is elsewhere.* We are the last of the living Surrealists.

(When YONI reaches the word "*Imagination*", MONI begins echoing him. When MONI reaches the name "Luis Buñuel", an audience member stands and also begins echoing. And when the audience member reaches the words "He crossed the line between art and politics…", a second audience member stands and begins echoing *him*. By the time the dancers near the end of their declaration, a third audience member interrupts.)

3RD AUDIENCE MEMBER: Psst. Get off the stage. Psst. Your time is up. Get off the stage.

Pause.

(YONI and MONI open their eyes and stare angrily at the third audience member. Then they look at one another.)

YONI AND MONI (mockingly): Psst. Get off the stage.

(They turn to the audience, put their thumbs on their noses, and wiggle their fingers, before exiting.)

SCENE THREE.

(A loud, deep voice is heard.)

VOICE: *LIFE IS A GIANT ASSHOLE WAITING TO TAKE A SHIT!*

YONI and MONI enter from opposite sides of the stage. Their backs are to the audience, and their hands are over their ears. Their legs are slightly spread, as if ready to take a shit.

They bend their knees, then straighten up, before turning and moving closer together. They repeat these movements (bending, straightening up, and turning), circling the stage. Once the circle is complete, they stop.

Pause.

SUDDENLY…the loud, fast polka music is once again heard.

There is an exact replay of the dance performed earlier. YONI and MONI, with their hands still on their ears, in unison, look left and right, and left and right again. YONI looks back left and is surprised to see MONI standing there. Both men do double takes and jump in fear.

The dancers begin hopping backwards, moving in opposite directions, shaking their fists up and down. Next, in an exaggerated walk, or perhaps jog, they crisscross, before spinning, with elbows out.

Finally, they hop out with their knees together, and their fingers in their noses. When they meet, MONI orders YONI to the ground, where he begins crawling back and forth like a dog, periodically lifting his leg to urinate, while MONI does a Russian dance, jumping and kicking, and ultimately hopping across the stage. At one point, YONI crawls through the hopping Moni's legs.

Suddenly...the music stops.

SCENE FOUR.

(YONI speaks directly to the audience.)

YONI: André Breton once said *the simplest surrealist act is to take a loaded handgun and fire aimlessly into a crowd.*

YONI and MONI remove pistols and begin firing into the audience. Once their assault is complete, they lift their weapons slowly to their heads.

Silence.

They pull the triggers, and with their opposite hands, mime the action of their brains being blown out.

The curtain falls.

SCENE FIVE.

Backstage.

(YONI and MONI are exhausted.)

YONI: It sure aint easy bein' a Surrealist, is it Moni?

MONI: It sure isn't, Yoni.

YONI: The public just doesn't want to break free from the chains of rationality.

MONI: It's Christianity, Yoni.

YONI: It's the bourgeoisie.

MONI: It's Capitalism.

YONI: And they'll never break free. (*Pause.*) It makes me feel old, Moni.

MONI: It makes me feel old, too, Yoni.

YONI: It makes me feel tired.

MONI: It makes me feel tired, too.

YONI: It makes me want…to dream.

MONI: It makes me…want to dream…too…Yoni.

(A bed appears, and YONI and MONI fall to sleep. Their heads meet together at the center of the bed, and they use each other's hands like pillows. Soft, angelic music is heard, as the two men peacefully rest.)

SCENE SIX.

The Dream, which is performed in slow motion.

YONI and MONI continue to rest.

In the shadowy light, a nun appears.

Silence.

The surrealist dancers rise slowly, looking upward in awe. They walk in opposite directions, circling toward the nun.

Pause.

The nun, who is visible only from the back, smiles and bows to YONI, and then to MONI. The dancers return bows, and then look at one another and smile.

Pause.

SUDDENLY... YONI and MONI begin beating up the nun. YONI punches her in the head, while MONI lands a blow to her belly. As the nun bends over in pain, MONI, holding his fists together high in the air, crushes her over her head. She falls to the ground, and the two men begin kicking her.

After an appropriate amount of beating, YONI and MONI begin laughing hysterically, holding their stomachs with their hands, and leaning backwards and forwards.

Eventually, they return to their bed and resume their previous positions. They continue to rest, the entire time smiling.

SCENE SEVEN.

The soft, angelic music continues to accompany the dancers' sleep. *Suddenly,* it comes to a halt.

NUN (in a man's voice): Get up! Come on, you guys. Get up! It's time for your next number!

(YONI and MONI awake.)

YONI: My god! Our number!

(Fauré's *Requiem* is heard, bursting through the theater.)

MONI: We forgot our number!

YONI: Hurry!

(The two men exit in a panic.)

SCENE EIGHT.

The Number.

As the *Requiem* builds in volume, the heads of various political and religious leaders through history fall from above. YONI and MONI burst forward carrying six foot long sticks. The ends of the sticks feature Styrofoam heads with nails poking out of the eyes. They jump around chaotically, crushing the heads, which explode like balloons.

The music gets faster and faster and faster…and then slower and slower and slower.

YONI and MONI begin to slow down, exhausted and out of breath. The music stops altogether, but the dancers continue crushing heads. Their old, surrealist bodies are wearing down.

YONI: What happened to the music, Moni?

MONI: I don't know, Yoni.

(They continue crushing heads, but in slow motion.)

YONI: I suddenly feel…weak.

MONI: I suddenly feel weak…too…Moni.

(They collapse.)

YONI: I feel like I want…to…dream.

MONI: I feel…like I…want…to…

Silence.

SCENE NINE.

(THE DOCTOR enters and, after examining the dancers, pronounces them dead. He turns and speaks directly to the audience.)

THE DOCTOR: There was a group of Surrealists…and now…they're all dead.

(He pauses, then exits.)

Silence.

The Song of the Open Road by Albert Hay Malotte is heard.

The nun and the doctor reappear, carrying large building blocks. They use these blocks to create a tomb, which they drag the bodies of YONI and MONI into. They enclose the tomb, and then set on top of it a picture frame, which contains a photo of the Surrealist group taken in 1929. All of the Surrealists, including Dalí, Buñuel, Magritte, Miro, Ernst, Breton, and Yoni and Moni themselves, are presented with their eyes closed.

The nun gently sets a pantyhose on the frame, and exits.

After several seconds, *The Song of the Open Road* fades.

Long Silence.

THE END

The Hobo Screenplay

A Silent Film Project by Todd Bash & Gustavo Octavio

(1989)

Characters

In order of appearance

Gus *a hobo*
The Hobo's Dog
A Man
An Old Hobo in the Park
The Film Director
The Film Crew
The Young Woman
The Cat Burglar
Policemen, Soldiers & Priests
A Nun
A Young Man
A Movie Studio Executive
2 Deformed Little Girls

SCENE ONE. Black & White. An empty field.

Fade up on a sign that reads: NO LOITERING, SLEEPING, MOVING OR BREATHING, AND DEFINITELY NO TRESPASSING. VIOLATORS WILL BE PROSECUTED AND BURNED IN HELL. On the lower right corner of the sign, in small letters, is a cross and the words: PROPERTY OF THE SAN GABRIEL VALLEY CHURCH OF CHRIST.

Pan down the pole of the sign to find a hobo (Gus) leaning, asleep. His dog, a little terrier, says good morning by licking Gus on his face. The hobo awakes, moving and blinking his eyes, and letting out a ferocious yawn.

Gus pats his dog affectionately on the head, but then is distracted by an enormous growl coming from his stomach. He looks down to his belly and begins rubbing it. Suddenly, he spots a paper bag lying nearby and excitedly grabs for it, removing what he hopes will be food. Unfortunately, it turns out to be a moldy sock. Gus makes several attempts to eat the sock, but after further consideration, decides to give it to his hound.

The hobo, who is wearing an old, dusty suit and bowler hat, stands up and begins preparing for his day: He stretches, rubs his aching back, straightens out his clothes, and quickly brushes his teeth with his bare finger. He is now ready to go to work.

Gus walks to a small tree where a little red wagon has been chained and locked. The wagon is filled with beautified garbage, including old electrical fans, car parts, and other trash, with little flowers growing out of them. The hobo looks around him carefully, making sure no one is watching, before undoing the lock by using a combination. He then sets the lock and chain in his wagon, puts a leash on his dog, and begins on his way. BUT...the wagon won't move. It's stuck. Gus pulls hard, straining his arm, to no avail. He examines the wagon closely, trying to uncover the problem. CLOSE-UP of a small crucifix lodged within one of the wheels. The hobo removes the crucifix and nonchalantly tosses it away. He then continues on his way, pulling his wagon in one hand, and his dog by the leash in the other.

The two walk into the distance, heading for the city.

SCENE TWO. Black & White.

CLOSE-UP of a sign that reads: NO DOGS ALLOWED. On the lower right corner in small letters is a cross and the words: PROPERTY OF THE SAN GABRIEL VALLEY CHURCH OF CHRIST.

Gus appears, tying his dog to the pole of the sign, which is situated near a street in a typical middle-class neighborhood.

The hobo walks up a pathway to one of the houses, pulling his wagon. He arrives at the front door and straightens up his suit before knocking. By the side of the door is a sign that reads: NO PEDDLERS.

The door opens and a man appears, wearing a rather large cross around his neck. He immediately slams the door on Gus.

CLOSE-UP of the hobo's foot stuck in the door, preventing it from closing.

The man reopens the door, with an annoyed look on his face. Gus pleads with him, explaining how he must sell his beautified objects in order to make a living. The man appears to be somewhat sympathetic, and shakes his head up and down, before going back into the house for a moment. Unsure of what the man is up to, Gus waits patiently. Finally, the man returns with a small pouch, which he happily hands over to the hobo. Excited, Gus accepts the pouch and turns to give a beautified fan in return. However, when his back is turned, the man slams the door shut on him. Startled, Gus jumps, and then pauses, wondering what's up. He examines the pouch more closely, and discovers it is empty. He turns it inside out, but nothing. Angry, Gus pounds on the door, but there is no answer. He continues pounding, until his hand is in pain. Dejected, he walks back down the pathway to the street, where he unties his dog and continues on his way.

SCENE THREE. Black & White.

A montage of shots showing one door slamming after another, after another, after another. Next, a series of shots showing the hobo's foot being smashed in a door again and again and again and again.

CLOSE-UP of the hobo's shoe. It disappears, and we see his bare foot, which is red, sore and swollen.

SCENE FOUR. Black & White. A park.

The hobo is seen leaning against a tree, rubbing and blowing on his sore foot. He then looks around him.

In the park, there are several hobos, all dressed like Gus, all with little wagons of beautified garbage, and all rubbing and blowing on their sore feet. Some sit on wooden benches, while others lie against trees.

One of these hobos, who is rather old, is desperately looking through a pouch for money. Excitedly, he removes a coin.

CLOSE-UP of the coin in the old hobo's hand. There is a little cross on it, and the word: VOID.

The old hobo, so shocked and disappointed, begins to cry uncontrollably. This leads to a heart attack.

The coin flips from the old man's hand, and rolls along the ground. It rolls all the way over to Gus, who picks it up, confused as to where it came from. After a moment, he spots the old hobo and walks to him. Gus bends over the old man, offering him the coin, but the man is too busy having a heart attack.

From the old hobo's POINT OF VIEW, Gus is seen from below, bending downward, holding out the coin...

SCENE FIVE. Color. A garbage dump.

A film director and crew are working. Over the director's shoulder, a massive heap of trash is seen, with naked corpses lying about. At the top of the heap, Gus (the actor) is bending over with a coin in his hand, just as he had done in the previous scene. There is a camera man underneath him, filming Gus from below. Beside them, a sound man is holding out a boom microphone.

The director yells "CUT" and the actor (Gus) and crew relax.

After the director gives some instructions to his actor, which Gus receives and understands, a crew member shouts "Quiet on the set", before the director yells "ACTION" and filming continues.

SCENE SIX. Black & White. The park.

Once again, from the old hobo's POINT OF VIEW, Gus is seen holding out the coin.

SCENE SEVEN. Color. The garbage dump.

The director shouts "CUT". Dissatisfied with how things are going, he makes his way up the garbage heap to Gus and begins discussing (arguing) the scene. He bends over, showing how he believes the actor should perform. While the director continues making his case, Gus suddenly spots something to the side. Deeply moved, he walks slowly toward an object, which he carefully picks up. It is a dead bird, which the actor holds gently in his hands, profoundly effected.

SCENE EIGHT. Color. An empty field, not far from where the film crew is shooting.

A young woman wanders through the field, surrounded by sheep. Her face is innocent, with tiny freckles on each side of her nose. She wears a tattered, brown dress.

SCENE NINE. Color. The garbage dump.

Gus remains entranced by the little, dead bird. After a moment, the director looks over to Gus. He walks up to the actor and pats him gently on the back. There is a long, tender silence between the two men.

SLOW FADE OUT.

SCENE TEN. Black & White.

Fade up on Gus (the hobo), who is pulling his wagon of beautified garbage down a street of houses. His dog follows close behind. It is now night, and he is exhausted.

As Gus passes one of the houses, he spots a cat burglar preparing to break in. The hobo taps the burglar on the shoulder, and warns him about the dangers of thievery. But the burglar ignores Gus, and continues with his foray.

The burglar opens a window and quietly climbs in.

SCENE ELEVEN. Black & White. Inside the house.

The burglar lights a candle to see in the dark. Suddenly, the lights go on, revealing a house full of people, most of whom are sleeping on the floor or on furniture. There are numerous policemen and soldiers, as well as a few priests and a nun. With complete calmness, the cat burglar moves backwards through the window and exits.

A knock is heard at the door. The nun opens it, revealing Gus outside, but for some reason she doesn't seem to notice him. She departs into another part of the house.

The hobo enters, bewildered by all of the sleeping bodies. He is startled when a young man storms in, smashing and stomping on a flugelhorn. The young man is wearing expensive slacks and a designer sweater, and has two small paintings, one by Hieronymus Bosch, and the other by Otto Dix, tied to his knees, dragging along the floor. Next to the young man is a small dog, also wearing designer doggie clothing.

Gus watches as the young man makes his way up a staircase. After a moment, he decides to follow him.

SCENE TWELVE. Black & White. A room upstairs.

Gus enters. The room's walls are covered with Hollywood movie posters and giant advertisements, including one for the San Gabriel Valley Church of Christ.

As Gus looks through the room, the young man suddenly appears from behind a curtain, pointing a pistol at Gus. Nervously, he orders Gus to move against a wall, and then demands to see his identification. When Gus explains that he doesn't have any, the young man grabs the hobo's bowler hat and tosses it out a window. Angered, Gus responds by ripping the young man's sweater from his body and doing the same. With a fiendish smile, the young man aims his pistol and fires, but instead of a bullet, a small grape falls from the weapon, landing on the floor. Outraged, the hobo knocks the pistol from the young man's hand, and begins smacking him across his face. In a frenzy, he then tears several of the posters and advertisements from the wall and throws them out the window.

SCENE THIRTEEN. Black & White. Outside the house.

The posters are seen falling from above and landing in a swimming pool, where the young man's sweater is floating, along with several rusted movie reels, dead birds, flugelhorns, and a naked corpse.

SCENE FOURTEEN. Black & White. Inside the upstairs room.

Gus begins to calm down. He is confused as to what has come over him, causing such a violent outburst. Suddenly, he turns around and discovers that he is surrounded by a mob of soldiers, policemen, priests, a nun, and the young man's dog. They charge the hobo, punching and slapping him, while the dog latches on to his buttocks. Finally, they lift him off the ground and hurl him out the window.

SCENE FIFTEEN. Black & White. Outside the house.

Gus falls from the window and splashes into the pool. Disoriented and bruised, he slowly makes his way to the edge of the pool, where he is greeted by his dog. He stands up, then grabs his hat from the water and rings it out.

After a moment, Gus notices someone is watching him.

SCENE SIXTEEN. Color. An empty field.

The young woman, surrounded by sheep, smiles at Gus.

SCENE SEVENTEEN. Black & White. Outside the house.

Gus smiles back, and then, timidly, reaches out his hand.

SCENE EIGHTEEN. Color. The empty field.

The young woman, somewhat unsure of what to do, eventually takes the hobo's hand.

SCENE NINETEEN. Black & White. Outside the house.

Gus and the young woman take the wagon with beautified garbage and begin walking down the street, hand in hand. His dog follows behind them.

Heading for home, they vanish in the night.

SLOW FADE OUT.

SCENE TWENTY. Color.

Fade up on a movie marquee. In giant letters are the words:

PREMIERE – NEW FILM BY OCTAVIO BASHKIEWICZ.

The director, Gus, and the rest of the cast and crew, are sitting outside the theater, looking sad and dejected.

Gus peeks through a door, inside the theater, where a house of empty seats can be seen.

After a moment, a movie studio executive (a rather obese man with a cigar in his mouth) appears. He grabs the director forcibly by his shirt, and demands that he turn in his union card. When the director removes his card from his wallet, the executive tears it up and tosses the pieces into the air.

As the executive departs, two deformed little girls appear, holding their tummies and laughing hysterically.

The director is shattered.

SCENE TWENTY-ONE. Color.

The director and his crew are walking alongside a barbed wire fence.

CLOSE-UP MOVING SHOT of the rusted barbed wire. Then...

LONG SHOT of the crew in the distance, walking closer and closer. Suddenly, JUMP CUT and they are once again far in the distance. As they continue to move closer, another JUMP CUT again places them far away. This pattern repeats, each JUMP CUT sending the crew further and further away, until, finally, they have completely disappeared.

Silence.

SCENE TWENTY-TWO. Color. The garbage dump.

The director appears, now a hobo himself, cold, hungry, and desperate. He begs an old lady for food, but the lady shuns him and spits in his face.

The director falls to his death, his body rolling down the giant trash heap.

LONG SHOT of the heap, littered with corpses, including many of the film crew members.

SCENE TWENTY-THREE. Color. The garbage dump.

CLOSE-UP of a book on Bertolt Brecht, lying among the trash. It is picked up and put into a sack where other books on Salvador Dalí, Karl Marx, and Sigmund Freud can be seen.

The sack is carried by the same young woman who had been wandering in the field of sheep. She is older now, dressed in cleaner clothes, and wears glasses.

The young woman walks through the dump, and notices an abandoned film camera. She picks it up and looks through the lens. As she continues walking, she films what she sees, capturing the heap littered with corpses. Eventually, she turns a corner and disappears.

Long Silence.

SLOW FADE OUT.

Seehunde

Musiktheater
Libretto by Todd Bash
Original Score Composed by Shigeru Kan-no
(2003)

Characters

The Young Man
Two Small Children *a boy and a girl*
A Homeless Man
A Man in his Thirties
A Little Boy
An Elderly Woman
A Soldier
An Old Man

1

An intense white light floods the stage.

Silence.

Random sounds are gradually heard, though they are distant and muffled.

Soon, the cries of seals are also heard, but in slow motion. Each moan is long and sustained, with an eerie, yet beautiful quality. They continue for several seconds.

As the seals' cries become more and more prominent, a new sound is introduced: A heavy, piercing wind.

The lighting darkens...

2

A cold, winter night. The landscape is covered in ice.
Upstage, the silhouettes of two young men appear. They are digging with shovels. The sound of their shovels plowing into the ice echoes through the night.

As the digging continues, a radio broadcast fades in and out, barely audible. It may or may not say the following:

RADIO BROADCAST: Les deux jeunes hommes sont payés une grande somme d'argent à creuser pour les os d'un playwright célèbre. Pour chaque objet façonné qu'lis découvrent...

After a moment, one of the young men sets down his shovel and makes his way down stage. The sounds of the windy night fade into the background...

3

A small storage room, lit only by a lantern.

The YOUNG MAN is taking a breather. He removes his cap and wipes some sweat from his forehead. He then takes a drink of water from his canteen.

The night is becoming quiet. Only distant animal sounds can periodically be heard. The lighting also changes, becoming darker, and filled with shadows.

Upstage, in the shadows, two small children appear, running through the night, carrying torches that flicker. They are naked, although it's difficult to see them in the darkness. Their giggles can be heard.

The children (a boy and a girl) eventually sit down on the cold ground. They begin touching each other's bodies for the first time, displaying a great deal of curiosity and innocence. Giggles continue to be heard.

After a moment, the sounds of the windy night return, and gradually get louder and more intense. The cries of seals also return. A collage of voices, barely audible and in different languages, follows. Some of the voices overlap each other.

FIRST VOICE: Laßt euch nicht verführen! Das Leben wenig ist...

SECOND VOICE: El mondo solo por el cielo solo dejándome la sangre por la escayola de los proyectos...

Historical recordings of speeches by Adolf Hitler and Joseph Stalin also fade in and out, along with the following sounds: Airplanes flying overhead; roaring thunder; children laughing; and a recording of Birgit Nilsson performing the Liebestod from *Tristan und Isolde*.

Meanwhile, the lighting has become an intense, fiery red.

The flood of sounds and lighting builds in intensity, before exploding with **CHAOS!** Dirt is hurled upon the stage, while buckets of red paint are splattered upon hanging muslin.

The vibrations from such an eruption continue for quite some time, before slowly withering away. Then...

Silence.

4

A small gloomy space, perhaps a cellar, or the crawl space under a house. Whispers in an unknown language can be heard, as well as periodic moans, and random sounds. Overall, though, there is a haunting sense of quiet.

During this scene, a number of episodes unfold simultaneously. The fiery red lighting remains, dark and with shadows.

The first episode reveals a homeless man who is lying in the dirt, barely able to move. He struggles to lift his arms and head, like an animal who has been wounded. The YOUNG MAN appears, watching from afar.

Second episode: Upstage, a MAN IN HIS THIRTIES is digging with a shovel. He uncovers several black trash bags, filled with garbage, which had been buried many years before. The bags are now decayed and covered with maggots.

Meanwhile, upstage left, an old baseball and three or four oranges roll upon the stage.

Third episode: A LITTLE BOY appears, playing with a grasshopper. He is on his knees covered with dirt.

Fourth episode: An ELDERLY WOMAN enters, with a large harness strapped around her shoulders. She is pulling a filthy bathtub that contains the following: Old toys; newspapers and magazines from the 1960s; pieces from a beat up lawn mower; and a typewriter from the 1920s.

The LITTLE BOY stands up and brushes the dirt from his jeans. He then makes his way to the bathtub, where he checks out some of the toys.

After a moment, the boy looks offstage and notices something that frightens him. He runs away, shouting, "*CUIDADO CON LA CARTERA! CUIDADO CON LA CARTERA!*" A soldier with a rifle storms in, and chases after the boy.

During these episodes, periodically, faint voices can be heard, speaking from some distance away. In addition, several rays of light, filtered through small, rectangular screens, cut into the space.

The YOUNG MAN wanders through the shadows, eventually

finding his way out of the crawl space. He follows a path which leads to a wooded area. The sound of running water is heard...

5

A river in the mountains. It is a quiet, moonlit night. An OLD MAN stands by a railing, looking down into the river. The lighting has faded into a peaceful blue.

The YOUNG MAN appears, and begins fishing with a rod he has found leaning against the railing. He casts his line into the river, and, after a moment, pulls in a giant squid. He tosses the squid aside, before trying again, with the same results. After pulling in three squids, the YOUNG MAN casts his line for a fourth try. This time he pulls in a baby.

The sound of an infant crying is heard for several seconds, before fading away.

The OLD MAN, moved by the sight of the baby, remembers a love he lost many years before. He begins singing...

OLD MAN: C'est l'enfant de mon amoureux, qui à gauche j'ici il y a tant d' années. I can still see her standing there, by the bridge, her body naked and unbathed, still a child herself. Her breasts were so soft and sweet. Und ihre Augen waren wie ein Rotwild braun. Ich glaubte kompletter Liebe innerhalb ich für sie. Les Montagnes ont été inondées par mon amour. But she left me...

Meanwhile, a MAN IN HIS THIRTIES appears opposite stage. He begins singing, along with the OLD MAN. The Old Man's voice fades, so now only the younger man is heard. He is telling the same story to a SMALL BOY.

MAN IN HIS THIRTIES: ...She left me because I am hideous. Non sono plù un giovane, ma un freak anziano, affrontante la morte. How I long for her softness to brush against my face. Cómo duelo para ver su sonrisa apenas una más vez...

The old man's voice is once again heard, while the younger man's voice fades.

OLD MAN: ...But I know I mustn't get my hopes up. The time is passing by faster than a meteor in space. My life is moving closer to its end. Se soltanto potessi vedere il suo un nuovo tempo giusto. If only I could touch her lips. Pero sé que la van. Y pronto, me irán, también.

The YOUNG MAN consoles the OLD MAN. After a moment, he gives him the fishing rod, before turning and walking away.

As the YOUNG MAN makes his way down the path, he spots the MAN IN HIS THIRTIES, along with the SMALL BOY, who are building a fort. The YOUNG MAN watches for several seconds, and then joins them. The sounds of their building, as well as the flowing river water, are heard.

LIGHTS SLOWLY FADE.

www.ingramcontent.com/pod-product-compliance
Lightning Source LLC
Chambersburg PA
CBHW020907080526
44589CB00011B/478